HISTORY AND RELIGION
AN UNCOMFORTABLE RELATIONSHIP

JOHN CUTTING

A GENTLY CYNICAL REFLECTION ON THE WAY
THE CHRISTIAN CHURCHES CAME ABOUT

ISBN: 978-1-7398203-1-2 (paperback)

ISBN: 978-1-7398203-0-5 (hardback)

History and Religion copyright © 2021 John Cutting

John Cutting asserts the right to be identified as the author of this work in accordance with the Copyright Designs and Patents Act 1988. All rights reserved.

No part of this publication can be reproduced or transmitted in any form or by any means, electronic, mechanical or otherwise, without the express written permission of John Cutting.

Cover design by Simon Emery

siemery2012@gmail.com

British Library Cataloguing in Publication Data
A CIP catalogue record for this book is available from the British Library

Some of the illustrations have been taken from my own photographs and some have been gathered from a variety of sources. If I have infringed anyone's copyright I offer my sincere apologies.

John Cutting

Cover illustration is drawn from the photograph of The Gallarus Oratory on page 80.

HISTORY AND RELIGION – AN UNCOMFORTABLE RELATIONSHIP

CONTENTS

AN INTRODUCTION 1
CHAPTER ONE 6
CHAPTER TWO - HISTORY, AND A BIT OF RELIGION 13
CHAPTER THREE - RELIGION, AND A BIT OF HISTORY 25
CHAPTER FOUR - THE BIBLE 32
CHAPTER FIVE - THE CHURCH 42
    ESSAY - CONSTANTINE 59
    ESSAY - AUGUSTINE 75
    ESSAY - HENRY VIII 86
CHAPTER NINE - SOME REFLECTIONS ON THE EARLY DAYS 100
CHAPTER TEN - AND ON THROUGH THE DARK TOWARDS THE MIDDLE AGES 115
CHAPTER ELEVEN - A TIME OF CHANGE 132
CHAPTER TWELVE - ENGLAND'S MOST IMPORTANT DAY 135
CHAPTER THIRTEEN - THE CHURCH IN NORMAN ENGLAND AND ON INTO THE PLANTAGENETS 142
CHAPTER FOURTEEN - MONEY AND REFORMATION . 161
CHAPTER FIFTEEN - SOME LEFT-OVER THOUGHTS ... 168
EPILOGUE 178
INDEX 183

LIST OF ILLUSTRATIONS

Stonehenge, Wiltshire, England......................................13
St. Peter's Basilica, Rome...40
Head of the Emperor Constantine...................................59
Nicaea..63
Nave of St Peter's Basilica..67
The Emperor Theodosius..69
Head of Christ (Mosaic Floor Panel)...............................77
The Gallarus Oratory..80
Stone huts on Skellig Michael..81
Catherine of Aragon...93
The Oseberg Ship...123
Fountains Abbey...157

By the same author: -

History and the Morris Dance

(A look at Morris Dancing from its earliest days until 1850)

Dance Books – Alton 2005

AN INTRODUCTION

King Herod died in the year 4 BC.
Four years later he 'sent forth and slew all the children that were in Bethlehem —'

(Matthew 2:16)

The calendar we all know, structured on BC/AD, was not devised until AD525 and Dionysius didn't get the start quite right. Thus Jesus was born in 4 BC. (Probably).

*****

This is a work of personal reflection.

Upon entering my ninth decade, after many years with a keen interest in both history and religion (but without any formal training in either) I felt the urge to highlight some of the influences that cross out of one and into the other. In the practical sciences we have managed to rid ourselves of the earth-centred universe that was once the teaching of the Church, but in history the ghosts are more subtle and some of them still live with us.

As a simple example, we tell our schoolchildren of the Viking raids on the monasteries of this country, starting at Lindisfarne in the year 793. We might go on to explain that the Vikings were after plunder, gold and silver for the melting pot. What we certainly do not tell them is how the wealth of the area came to be concentrated in the house of men who had taken a vow of poverty. Or again, many of us will feel uncomfortable if we learn that the meal we have just finished contained horse meat. Food labelling is a modern idea, but there is a shadow that reaches far back into the past. Pope Hadrian I told us in the year 786 that eating horse meat was the mark of a pagan.

To start the writing of a book on theology for fun is probably a rare event. But perhaps I should explain that what I mean by 'fun'

AN INTRODUCTION

is 'without the stiff shirt, the soap box and the pompous attitude'. The seriousness of the content is for you to judge. The words 'personal reflection' in my opening line are also important. What follows is based on books I have read, lectures I have attended and on my own attempts to stitch the whole thing together — there are no new discoveries and all the facts are fairly easy to check — the only originality comes in where to place the emphasis. I have consulted with no one, so the usual claim that any remaining errors are my own is painfully true. But then, all the good bits are mine, also!

I am taking advantage of present day freedom to write about religion without restriction, but I am well aware that there are many people out there for whom religious beliefs are of extreme importance. To such people, should they read this book, I hope they will see it as a light hearted tossing around of old ideas. Whether you see this modern freedom as an advance, or as a retrograde step: we will see.

At the very start, I should perhaps confess to uttering harsh words against the Roman Catholic Church. This is not so much about their theology, more about their attempts at World Domination. In the present day, I have many friends who are happy to order their lives according to the rules of the Roman Catholic Church, and I have no wish to influence them. But we, nevertheless, ought to remember that from the year 381 until Henry VIII walked down the aisle with Anne Boleyn, Rome made a pretty good job of controlling what England thought.

Here, then, are some organisational thoughts about this book. Firstly, there is a recent move to change the letters BC (Before Christ) to BCE (Before the Christian Era) and to change AD (Anno Domini, the year of our Lord) to CE (Christian Era). I see this as a rather distasteful current fashion for political correctness which I shall not be following. On a rather more serious note, I freely acknowledge that half the world's population is female, but if I write "he and she", "hers and his" whenever appropriate in the text, it interrupts the flow, so I hope you will agree with my claim that

AN INTRODUCTION

the "male" embraces the "female". Thirdly, I dislike having to hunt for notes at the back of a book, so there won't be any.

In a work of personal reflection, it is only fair that you, the reader, should have some idea of the person doing the reflecting.

> Born in Harrow, Middlesex, England, in 1931, to a mother who had a warm feeling towards the Church of England and a father whose leading interest was the Territorial Army which, in those days, involved a certain amount of church attendance. As a child, I remember a tea-party on the vicar's lawn and joining the cubs (junior scouts) attached to a nearby church. Then all this stopped with the outbreak of war in 1939 and life became very different.
>
> Leaving school in 1948 and heading towards civil engineering, I was advised not to go to university as universities were intended for doctors, teachers, lawyers and men intending to enter the church. (I must have been among the last people to receive such advice.)
>
> This last point has some relevance to my present theme. Until the Second World War, the universities could be seen to have two primary functions: firstly, to educate the sons of the upper crust to suit them for management (for estates, for industry, for the colonies, or for this country itself) and secondly, to provide the church with a constant flow of clergymen. As with all generalities, this is not entirely true, but the underlying idea is worth a thought
>
> Today I see myself standing on the sidelines of the Church of England — the best fit for the society in which I live.

That last sentence is easily read, but it leads us gently into deep water. Does religion exist to fit a society, or should the society be adapted (or even pushed) to fit the religion? Indeed, what is religion?

AN INTRODUCTION

Take a book: ink and paper and a bit of glue. Very much something in the material world. Stand before a judge and swear to tell the truth, the whole truth, and nothing but the truth, and the book you hold might become something different. For me, religion is about this difference. Were someone to burn the book, a lot of anger would be released. Is this anger part of religion?

Christianity had its beginnings in a country under military occupation at the right-hand end of the Mediterranean. Islam started among desert traders in Arabia. Yet both religions are now widespread in the very different conditions of the modern world. Both have struggled to increase their areas of influence, and gone through many battles and much bloodshed on the way, and they have both been accompanied by endless theological arguments and divisions.

So, is society pressed into a fit with religion, or is religion adapted to suit the society? It has to be a bit of each — but don't tell anyone!

The title of this book, 'History and Religion — an Uncomfortable Relationship', arose from a feeling that each influences and the other but, generally speaking, we try not to notice. We might talk about King David, but we need to change hats if we then want to mention the Late Bronze Age. Similarly, the Good Book tells us about the Philistines, indeed we still use the word to mark someone as rough and barbaric, but archaeology shows us the Philistines as the up and coming new people with their Iron Age technology: the shape of progress. Not the old stick-in-the-muds with King David.

For sixteen hundred years people have been combing their way across the Near East looking for physical evidence to support the Bible stories and, bearing in mind the huge effort, with very little success. Although, on second thoughts, one should perhaps mention a huge tourist industry with guides telling stories and two manufacturing industries; one producing mementoes for the tourists, and one making 'genuine artefacts' for wealthy collectors. In my more cynical moments I think of Constantine's mother in Jerusalem, seeking the 'True Cross' — "Yes, madam, how many would you like?"

CHAPTER ONE

The trigger that started this book into writing lies in three statements.
Statements that are common currency in the world of history books and television.
Statements that have irritated me for forty years and more.
Statements that offer the bare minimum of information — then slam the door shut!

> Statement 1 — "Constantine was the first Christian Emperor."
> Statement 2 — "Augustine brought Christianity to Britain in AD 597."
> Statement 3 — "Henry VIII was fed up with Queen Catherine who had failed to give him a son and he fancied Anne Boleyn as a replacement, but the Pope wouldn't give him a divorce. So Henry broke with Rome and England became protestant."

Each statement will have its own chapter, in due course. (Although placed as chapters later in this book, they can be read separately as independent essays.)

*****

Many years ago, I recall listening to a radio programme, 'Gardener's Question Time', in which Professor Alan Gemmell said to a young questioner, "You asked me a 'Why' question and I gave you a 'How' answer." A splendidly compact reference to the world we all face. Ask how does a seed grow and modern science will give you a detailed explanation. But ask why does it grow and the only really satisfactory response is that God designed it so that it would. Perhaps the world is divided into the material and the spiritual according to how we ask the question. Are bread and wine at a dinner party different from bread and wine in front of an altar? If transubstantiation works, why is there an option of wafers with gluten-free flour?

Enough of the questions! We clearly live in a scientific world where many actions and reactions are fairly obvious: drive your car for long enough and the fuel will run out. Devote your mind to faith, hope and charity and the following consequences are more difficult to foresee. It could be argued that human development has seen some things drift from the spiritual world over into the scientific: once the weather was under the control of Zeus or Jupiter — now we can get close to understanding the weather through the Met Office supercomputer, although it doesn't stop us praying for good weather. The story of life and death was once entirely in the hands of God, but now we have the National Health Service. You can, of course, argue that the supercomputer and the NHS are themselves part of God's work, but this points us down a path to where all responsibility is handed over to God and the human brain can go to sleep. But surely, the unique function of the God-given human brain is to think?

And yet, as a footnote, most of us will be aware that the organised church has had a lot of trouble over the years with people who think. But they did have a solution — pass the matches!

Religion is about a Man/God relationship — at least, it is for me. The concept of God being eternal works well in Genesis but simply does not fit against a background of present scientific thought. God as Conductor of the Big Bang thirteen and a half billion years ago, then waiting around for the earth to solidify before getting the geological periods in the right order — no, it doesn't work for me. The 'eternity' of the Man/God relationship can only begin when human thought comes on the scene. If God does have a relationship with things on earth before man, or with beings on other planets, then this is something I am not equipped to comprehend.

CHAPTER ONE

Which brings us to God Himself. If you read 'God made man in His own image,' then there is a clear match between the appearance of God and the appearance of a man. Most of us will feel fairly comfortable with a picture of God as an elderly man with a grey beard and wearing a white nightshirt (and, if you are under twelve, sitting on a fluffy cloud). On the other hand, if you use a different translation and see God as making man in His imagination, then there is no need for any similarity of appearance between God and man, and God can look like anything you fancy — a green dragon — a girl in a mini skirt — No! Sorry! That's going too far. But this is, of course, all nonsense. This is man creating God in his own imagination, not the other way around. When we come to Jesus Christ the question of appearance is not a problem. There must be a fair number of men around today, born thirty years ago in Bethlehem to local parents, who look very like Jesus.

The words 'image' and 'imagination' in the above paragraph serve as an important reminder of how dependant we are on translation. There was, of course, no such thing as an English language in biblical times, so people like me, who can read nothing else, depend on translators. It is often said that translators work with divine guidance, but to translate Aramaic or Syriac and Hebrew into Greek, then into Latin, then into English takes an awful lot of divine guidance. I am told that to read St Paul's letters in his own rather earthy Greek is a very different experience to reading Jerome's tidied up versions in Latin.

Somewhere around 1954, I was at an evening class in archaeology when we were told about some early biblical writings recently discovered inside a crocodile — the stuffing inside a taxidermised crocodile. More recent years have filled out this story. The ancient town of Oxyrhynchus, 160 km south of Cairo, had a rubbish dump in which were deposited enormous quantities of written material; the durable nature of papyrus, together with the hot dry climate of Egypt, meant that much was still legible. Excavations had started in 1896 and continue to this day, with 75 volumes published so far. The initial enthusiasm was a hunt for lost works from classical Greek authors, but in more recent years popular interest has turned toward material related to the Bible.

About 300 km further south along the Nile, at a site now called Nag Hammadi, a large clay pot with a lid was discovered in 1945. It contained thirteen leather bound books, or codices, written in the Coptic language, mostly translations from the Greek. These books were assorted writings from the fringes of Christian theology. One of the pieces has become fairly well known, 'The Gospel of Thomas', a collection of the sayings of Jesus.

> His disciples said to him, "When will the kingdom come?" "It will not come by watching for it. It will not be said, 'Look, here it is', or 'Look, there it is.' Rather, the Father's kingdom is spread out upon the earth, and people do not see it."
>
> (Saying 113)
>
> "— For what goes into your mouth will not defile you; rather, it is what comes out of your mouth that will defile you."
>
> (Saying 14)
>
> Jesus said, "Become passers-by."
>
> (Saying 42)

Judas Thomas is referred to as the twin of Jesus: if this were biologically true, it would put a very different slant on the Christmas story.

A couple of things really need to be said at this point. Firstly, the desert sands of Egypt had become home for Christian monks and hermits in the third and fourth centuries. (The essay on Augustine gives some background to these Desert Fathers.) And the Greek spirit of theological debate was still raging, where last year's orthodoxy could very easily become this year's heresy. Thus it seems quite likely that the Nag Hammadi pot stored material that had fallen out of favour. A second point is really a gentle warning. We in the twenty-first century are completely separated from the Greek world of hot theological debate. Then, of course, all material was hand written and therefore rare, and some of it was even marked 'secret'. In many ways you will find a strange land, with a number of characters you will not have met before. Valentinus has a Christian following in pursuit of a deeper spiritual knowledge, and Seth and Sophia seem to play important parts. One book has the splendidly obscure title, 'The Discourse on the Eighth and Ninth'. It concerns a dialogue between thrice-greatest Hermes and a student, concerning the higher levels of spiritual enlightenment. If you choose to enter this world of Gnostic writings and other 'wisdom' literature, keep a firm grip on your sense of reality.

If we go back for a moment, to the late nineteenth century, a book with close similarities to the, yet to be discovered, Nag Hammadi material, was sold in Cairo to a German scholar. This book is now referred to as the Berlin Gnostic Codex. It includes a fragmentary text, 'The Gospel of Mary' (of Magdala) which includes a surprising statement from Jesus; "There is no such thing as sin." — people create sin by mingling inappropriately with the world. It is made clear that Mary had full membership among the disciples, indeed, some have seen her as their leader, at least in matters of spiritual understanding. Mary tells of a vision of the soul's ascent through darkness, desire and ignorance to liberation and rest.

> What binds me has been slain, and what surrounds me has been destroyed, and my desire has been brought to an end, and ignorance has died. In a world I was set loose from a world — The chain of forgetfulness is temporary. From this hour on, for the time of the due season of the age, I will receive rest in silence.
>
> (BGC 16-17)

CHAPTER ONE

Even without fully understanding it, it is clear that this is teaching at a high level and it is probably even better in Greek. Words of this sort presumably reached Pope Gregory the Great (590-604) and clashed with his ideas for the growing Catholic Church, where religious teaching was a male-only preserve and the Church had an aim to embrace all people. A story was put about that Mary of Magdala was a retired/reformed prostitute and her appearance in religious writing was steered towards the practical domestic matters that were the proper concern for a woman.

Before leaving this Gnostic material, it is perhaps worth taking note that here we see a very different sort of religion: a very different sort of Christianity. Indeed, one might go further and picture a fundamental style of religion concerned with the growth of the human mind, soul and understanding, to which you could simply add a colour; Christian, Buddhist, Confucian or what you will. Mary's 'rest in silence' sounds very close to the Buddhist 'Nirvana': 'absorption into the supreme spirit' as my dictionary has it.

Should we perhaps be looking for two different ways in which religion can be used? The Desert Fathers and Mary's Gospel point to a full-time activity: study and personal development to a point where you pass through personality and out the other side to a wider world. More familiar to most of us will be the religion of the instruction manual — do this; do that; don't do that. So long as religion and government adjust their instruction manuals to some sort of fit, we can hope for a happy land. Something along these lines must have been in Gregory's mind: Mary was clearly running along a very different track.

At about the same time as the Nag Hammadi find, written material was found in various caves near the Dead Sea. From 1946, over the next ten years, hundreds of pieces of parchment were discovered. Some were actual texts from the Bible and others seem to relate to a religious community. These writings date widely, from the fifth century BC to the fourth century AD and Wikipedia tells us there were 972 texts in total. This material needed a great deal of work, fitting together thousands of fragments, then conservation and translation, work that was undertaken by a team of Roman Catholic priests and academics. As time went on, it became increasingly obvious that the Church of Rome was holding on to this material with grim determination. Pleas from non-Catholics to have a look were rejected. It took forty long years before the Dead Sea Scrolls and the translations were released from the grip of the Catholic Church, and the release was accompanied by a statement that, 'There was nothing in this material that conflicted with Roman Catholic theology' — now there's a surprise! But surely those forty years must suggest a mousehole of doubt in the ironclad certainty of the Catholic Church?

CHAPTER TWO
HISTORY, AND A BIT OF RELIGION

So what of history? Many thousands of years ago, a primitive man expended energy dragging a half-eaten carcass back to his cave because he knew that there would be a tomorrow. The start of planning for the future, a very human characteristic. To a hunter-gatherer, living on what he could find, and ranging across large areas of land, it was important to remember what grew where and when it came into fruit. To pass such information on to his children would lead to an expansion of language. Sitting round a fire in the evening, it is easy to imagine stories being told of past experiences, of that nasty lot that lived on the other side of the river, and a warning to avoid a particular cave haunted by an evil spirit.

All fiction, of course: it will be another five thousand years and more before anyone can write. But it all seems very plausible and it suggests that both history and religion may have occupied the human mind for a very long time.

Stonehenge, Wiltshire, England

HISTORY, AND A BIT OF RELIGION

Sitting in a Mesolithic hut on a summer's evening, talk might well range over which bushes were showing signs of a good crop this year, and wondering why there weren't as many deer around these days. Well known tales might be told of their father's father stealing a wife from a distant tribe. Then a flash and a bang as a thunderstorm reminds them that there are things outside their understanding. A cow in a thunderstorm just gets wet: a man in a thunderstorm asks: Why? Who? And before long we have a thunder god. Now whether you, today, consider this thunder god to be a rather childish pagan idea, or whether you consider it to be 'our' God presenting Himself in a form understandable to a primitive mind, I leave it to you to decide. Taking a further step, is 'God' our way of explaining the inexplicable? Both then and now? If so, do we see religion in a natural decline as an understanding of the material world expands?

Years ago, an archaeologist coming across a hole in the ground might describe it as a 'ritual pit': using the word 'ritual' to signify something that is clearly important, but whose purpose we do not understand. Get out of the car and look at Stonehenge and the word 'ritual' may well come into your mind.

'Of, or pertaining to a rite' as a dictionary might put it, 'ritual' carries hints of strange and mysterious goings-on without the usual restraint of every day common sense. A ritual is therefore an outward and visible display with an underlying rite. Marriage is the rite: the church service and the food and drink afterwards are the ritual. This relationship between an underlying idea and an outward show has caused many problems. Indeed, it could be seen that the simple transfer of an idea into words is a first step away from the purity of the thought. A second step away is when those words are put into writing. A third step away is when someone else reads those words. Call the words Holy Scripture and we begin to have some sympathy with the problems faced by the Church.

HISTORY, AND A BIT OF RELIGION

One man of faith, or perhaps the mind of one man of faith, has contact with God. He understands. He stands under God. No words are required. The Buddhists call it 'Enlightenment'. If he wishes to communicate this state of the good, disciples may sit at his feet, coming under discipline.

Turn your mind now to the Church of Christ. I have little doubt that the end objectives are the same, but the method is now mass production. Publish a teaching. Train teachers. Send them worldwide. There are few of us able to stand unaided under God, so the Church offers help. Faith. Faith in Jesus; faith in Holy Mary, Mother of God; faith in the words of Holy Scripture and faith in the Church. With faith, even the simplest of men can come to God.

With such large-scale objectives, the Church could not avoid contact with the material world; books, transport, buildings and, most importantly, money. Books give power to those who can read them: grand buildings attract the pilgrims, but where do the poor live? Money is created by those who produce: how does it move from the field and the workshop into the Church?

This is not intended as criticism: it is the way the world works. But justice depends upon proportion, and for a thousand years the Church fixed the rates. So thoughts of God reach the mind of man through an entanglement of Church organisation.

Back in the fourth century, between the Council of Nicaea in 325 and the Council of Constantinople in 381, the Christian Church was getting itself into shape. (The essay on Constantine will give a few more details). Trying to take a simple and a detached view, Nicaea saw Christians released from their earlier persecution and oppression; they had become legitimate. Constantine started the building of notable churches, Bishops became leaders of society and the administrative structure we still think of as 'The Church' was built up. For many, the freedom to be a Christian was reward enough, and the Church was there to help them along their way. However, the Council of Constantinople a few decades later changed the atmosphere; the sense of freedom faded; the Church and the State came close together and unless you followed their rules, you were not a Christian. The Church moved from the Greek world into the more disciplinarian atmosphere of Rome and took an even firmer grip on Christian affairs. A subtle change had taken place: the Church now saw itself as the Prime Distributer and the only true access to Christianity. Of all human organisations, it was the most important.

But not everybody agreed. Did not the Gospels tell of Jesus and the Disciples living a life at subsistence level? Yet Church leaders now live in palaces! Communion first took place in an ordinary room in a house so why do we now need grand churches decorated with gold? Discontent along these lines may well have started early: we begin to get signs surviving from the fourteenth century.

A recent biography of John Wycliff by Gillian Evans paints an interesting picture of Oxford University in the 1300's. It shows how 'education' and 'Roman Catholic teaching' had come very close to being the same thing. Oxford was under the authority of the Bishop of Lincoln, who in turn was under the Pope. But, happily, Oxford was a long way from Lincoln so perhaps the control was not as tight as some churchmen would have wished.

Today we all have a strong feeling for the physical world (I must pay that gas bill; I need some more socks). Religion is a bit of a sideline; perhaps an hour on Sunday, or thoughts at the funeral of a friend in the village. In the fourteenth century, we are told, matters were quite the reverse. People were daily concerned about their eternal souls, perhaps planning a pilgrimage to a shrine in order to touch the bones of a saint, put money in the box and get some relief from this damned rheumatism. Even the material task of planting seeds was so that God would provide food in the autumn. If I might whisper a word of caution at this point: in the fourteenth century the great majority were illiterate, thus any written record or history must come down to us from the hand of those who could write: lords, estate managers and, yes, you've got it, the Church!

If we think about the Church for a moment, just before and just after the Black Death in the fourteenth century, the Church had been working on the human mind and soul for a thousand years. What was the state of play? Had the Church managed to mould mankind to its liking? Or had mankind been made of sterner stuff and pushed the church into an adjustment of teaching that the human mind was more prepared to accommodate? So long as we are talking theology, there are no real answers to these questions — they remain debating points. But, of course, mankind and the Church are not separate: the Church is staffed by mankind, and together with mankind, the Church has needs and ambitions in the material world. At this point let us go back to Oxford University.

The word 'university' carries the sense 'all of us', a group of people, teachers and students, with a common purpose: and underlying this purpose is a World View. It is probably fair to say that the only world view available from fourteenth century Oxford was the Roman Catholic one. Advance in the spiritual sense, and also in the material world were both seen to come from study at the University. With a first degree you could become a priest, with a second, a bishop and from there, doors were opened into real areas of power and wealth around the King. But study was never easy. A first degree, covering Grammar, Logic, Rhetoric, Arithmetic, Music, Geometry and Astronomy would take seven or eight years (which, if you started at fourteen, would get you a degree in your early twenties, much the same as today). Then a second degree in Medicine, Law or Theology (where Medicine was a very minor partner: Canon Law and Theology ruled the roost). Ten or twelve years out of the shorter lifespan expected in those days, ten or twelve years paying for your food and lodging in Oxford, plus tuition and examination fees. A near impossible challenge for any man without substantial family wealth behind him, unless — unless he was a member of a religious order. Benedictine and Cistercian monks, Dominican and Franciscan friars had all taken a vow of poverty and thus had no money. But this vow of poverty was personal; it did not extend to their parent Houses — indeed, the

Monasteries and Friaries were raking it in! Bequests, donations and rents, together with collections from a variety of sources and a good share of the tithe payments, these Religious houses were buying up land and property and ever increasing their rent income.

The monks and friars had also taken a vow of obedience, so when their House sent them to university — they went — all charges paid for. Indeed, by this time, the religious institutions owned houses and halls within Oxford, so food and lodging were all provided by the Company (sorry, a slip of the pen). We have no figures to suggest what proportion of Oxford students were attached to the religious houses as monks and friars (sorry, nuns, or women of any sort, didn't get a look in for another six hundred years). I would personally guess that half to three quarters of all students were Religious. The way the financial structure was loaded being the basis for my guess.

So, looking from one side, we have a University arranging its courses to suit its best customers. From the other side, the Religious Houses could see great advantages in having their staff (another slip) educated to a level at which they could give direction to the common people, and the best students might even find their way to become close advisors to the King and thus influence matters in the Church's favour. A materialistic assessment, but then we all live in a material world. Yet much emphasis was placed by everybody on doing the work of God. One feels tempted to wonder what God thought of the system?

It has to turn on the awkward question of how closely did the teachings and behaviour of the fourteenth century Roman Church serve the best interests of a) God, and b) Man? This is clearly dangerous territory. I am not sure whether it makes sense to talk to God having interests: God is just God. God said 'Let it be', and it was! Now, did God create Man and then let him loose to get on with life unaided, albeit with a bit of additional guidance around AD30? Or was God sitting on the panel that established the Rules of Oxford University? OK, I know the words are silly, but there is an important idea underneath. What, then, of the Church? I am sure that any good Catholic would claim that the 'best interests' of the Church and the 'best interests' of God are the same thing. But then, I am not a Catholic. It seems clear that the educational system at Oxford was in close conformity with what the Church wanted. Therefore, in continuation of the question above, we can confirm that the fourteenth century Roman Church served the best interests of c) The Roman Church. This statement is not quite as cynical as it might at first seem. For nearly a thousand years the Roman Church had held a dominant position in what Europeans called 'the known world'. Thus, for ninety-nine percent of the people, this world and the next were just as the Roman Church described them. There was no other picture available. Occasional stirrings by other ideas were quickly labelled witchcraft or heresy and heavily suppressed. Thus man, God, the Church and Oxford University all followed the same path: the only path!

But not everything in the garden was rosy: there were early signs of discontent. Why were peasants hungry and bishops fat? It didn't seem to fit in with the Bible stories. Or again, the Church taught that after death you'd spend time in Purgatory — unless you had paid money to the Church to counterbalance your sins. Yet nowhere in the Bible could you find this idea. It is convenient to suggest that these unsettling ideas came out of the social upheaval that followed the Black Death of 1349 — it might even be true. But in any case, the connection between the Church and money was becoming clearer.

England's first popular author, Geoffrey Chaucer, was also active in this second half of the fourteenth century and while there may be few who have read 'The Canterbury Tales' from cover to cover, many will have heard about the scurrilous verbal conflict between a Friar and a Summoner. (There is a nest ordained for friars under Satan's tail!) And also about the cynical exploitation of religion by the sales of Papal Indulgencies, Pardons and Relics. There is also much about true devotion to God, although the Canterbury pilgrims usually saw this as a direct man to God relationship, rather than one mediated by the Church hierarchy.

HISTORY, AND A BIT OF RELIGION

So, had there ever been a time when the English people, and indeed the whole of Europe, followed the Roman Church with sheep-like obedience? I don't know, but if it had ever been true, then by the late 1300's, there was a cold draught of cynicism in the air.

This same period also saw trouble within the Papacy. The year 1378 was the start of the 'Great Schism': Urban VI was elected, then his election was challenged and Clement VII was elected: two popes, each excommunicating the other. Urban was politely described as having an 'unstable temperament' although 'mad' is a shorter word. This schism went on with a sequence of conflicting Popes for nearly forty years, with full Papal establishments at both Rome and Avignon and, occasionally, Pisa. All very expensive. By the time of Pope John XXIII (the first one), who became Pope with military support in 1410, there were three Popes. (John had spent his early life as a pirate!) It was Pope John who called the Council in Rome that excommunicated Jan Hus and condemned the writings of the Oxford scholar John Wycliff. Their crimes had been their suggestion that the Church should follow a simple style of life as portrayed in the Bible. Clearly, the Church saw its position in a very different light.

The essay on Constantine talks about the early days of Christianity and the widespread conflict between different versions of theology. Nicaea (325) defined the path that Christianity was to follow, then Constantinople (381) banned everything else. Thus the Roman Church of the fourteenth century had behind it the comfort of a thousand years of theological certainty. Out of this certainty had grown intolerance. As a schoolboy once translated 'Dieu et Mon Droit' — 'My God I am right!'

Bishop Ambrose of Milan, back in the fourth century, had worked hard at an attempt to establish the authority of the Church and its bishops above that of the Emperor. Nine hundred years further on, many of the fourteenth century Popes were trying for the same objective: to give Popes authority above the Kings and Emperors of the material world. Whilst the Popes never quite achieved superiority in the political sense, in the financial world they did pretty well and funds flowed across Europe and into the Papal coffers.

Early in the Old Testament we meet a simple tale of good and evil; God and a serpent in the Garden of Eden. For some reason that I only partially understand, this two-part framework fell out of favour. I think the problems arose because the two elements came to be seen as equal and opposite — a Good Empire and an Evil Empire — with the Good Empire being Heaven and the Land of God; and all the material world seen as a creation of the Devil. I suspect we may be seeing ideas brought over from older, more primitive religions. Anyway, these ideas came to be called 'dualist', and to the Catholic Church, 'dualist' was bad. The Church didn't like the Gnostic writings, either; so Gnostic writing came to be seen as 'dualist'. There is a suggestion that a Gnostic group was divided into two-parts — those who 'knew' and those who did what they were told. Perhaps the Catholic Church found this embarrassing. I do wonder whether this anti-dualistic feeling went back as far as the Council of Nicaea. Is this, perhaps, why the Trinity became so surprisingly important?

Somewhere around the middle of the tenth century, an obscure group of people in an obscure location seem to have become a centre for dualist thought. The Bogomils of Bulgaria sound a bit like a circus troupe, but they appear to be the source of that rather unpleasant word 'Buggery'. Bogomil dualist thinking became a powerful force in Southern France, in the country around Toulouse in the late twelfth century, taking the name 'Cathar'. The Cathars had a good answer to that age-old question, "I lead a good life and do all I can to promote God's work, and yet the world treats me badly?" The Cathar answer was that the material world was the work of an evil creator, into which the spiritual world had become entangled. They also had difficulty in relating the God of the Old Testament to the God in the New Testament.

Pope Innocent III (1198-1216) led the Catholic opposition to this heresy. Innocent was a bit of an enthusiast for crusading; he had launched the Fourth Crusade which captured (Christian) Constantinople and he had even threatened England's King John with a crusade. Then in 1208, he organised what came to be called the Albigensian Crusade against the Cathar heretics (offering the usual remission of sins for those who took part) and demonstrated the rightness of Catholic theology by extensive slaughter and burnings. But before we tip up our noses in a 'holier than thou' attitude, we should remember that we still send soldiers off to fight for what we believe to be right. 'The Defence of Western Democracy' may have replaced 'The Crusade', but the dead are just as dead. We would also do well to remember that for a thirteenth or fourteenth century European, a threat to the unity of Catholic thinking would seem to be more than a threat to life — it was a threat to the life hereafter — the prospect of eternity in hell. For so he had been told.

Anyone who has looked at old religious paintings either on canvas or on church walls will be aware that Catholic art contained a generous helping of devils. Now, there must have been a difference between the 'Evil Empire' half of a dualist world, and the battalion of devils employed by the Catholic God to torture dead sinners — but I'm afraid I can't see it.

After these ramblings through the thirteenth and fourteenth centuries, what can we say to tidy up some of the loose ends? It is clear that the Roman Catholic Church was very large, very powerful and very rich. It had set up a grand building in every single village of the land to tower over the villagers, both physically and spiritually. It had installed a team to teach in every parish and to ensure that everybody followed the path as set out by the Church. It controlled a University to teach the teachers. In modern political language, it was totalitarian government. It waved the big stick of eternal damnation and any whisper of opposition did not last long. I feel sure that the Church had inherited much of this flavour of command and control from our Viking/Norman invaders of 1066. (It should perhaps be noted that the wild and violent Vikings who raided monasteries and killed monks had converted themselves into

Roman Catholic followers of the Pope, for reasons that are seldom examined.)

Two questions come to mind. Firstly, how had this situation come about? And secondly, what part did religion play in a Church that looked increasingly like a government department?

Many books of history accept this picture of the medieval church as a starting point: as something that emerged fully-formed out of the mists of the Dark Ages. In a very quiet voice I would like to offer another way of looking at it. The Dark Ages, I suggest, were created by the Christian Church! Not, perhaps, as a deliberate act, more as a by-product of the Council of Constantinople in 381. (The essay on Constantine gives a little more detail.) The Churches' single-minded concentration on Nicaea and the Trinity, together with its rejection of all other knowledge, ideas and discussion gave us the Dark Ages. After a thousand years of enforcing a one-track mind, it is not surprising that there was little opposition.

But one thing was beginning to shake the foundations — money! The Church had always needed money: at the beginning someone had to buy the bread and the wine; as numbers increased, some place of assembly was needed, and then the bishop needed a distinctive cape. Given the widespread devotion to the Church, raising money was not difficult, and as time went on, moneymaking schemes, both official and unofficial took on a theological colour: your future in the next world depended on the size of your contribution. Where money-raising was easy, it was difficult to resist the cry of 'More!' Better than money was land: for land gave you a yearly income. The Church acquired more and more land. The yield from land depended on what you did with it, so, out with the village and the villagers with their messy and small time farming — and in with sheep! The Bishop of Winchester owned land on London's South Bank — the most profitable use? The Ladies of the Night were called 'Winchester Geese'.

As a footnote, in my own lifetime, I can recall an outcry in the newspapers (somewhere in the 1950's) when it was discovered that a range of properties in Bayswater, much used by prostitutes, was in fact owned by the Church of England.

Back in the fourteenth century, we can begin to get some feeling for the discontent expressed by Jan Hus and John Wycliff, and for the wry humour of Geoffrey Chaucer. Here, indeed, are the seeds of the Reformation, a hundred and fifty years before Anne Boleyn came on the scene. The Reformation had little to do with religion, or theology, or even about Henry's divorce. The Reformation was about money. How to stop the drift of the World's Wealth into the hands of the Church. Or, more specifically, towards Rome and into the hands of the Pope.

A page or so back, I asked, 'what part did religion play?' A difficult question. Had the question been, 'what part did the Church play?', then the answer would have been simple, 'very great!' But we are faced with a contentious issue: how much religion was there in the fourteenth century Church? If the Church issued an instruction; was that God speaking? In all honesty, I don't think we can get very far with this matter; the modern mind is so far distant from that of an illiterate fourteenth century peasant.

Wearing my slightly cynical hat, was not this peasant intimidated by the Church into believing that the Church was religion: indeed, that the Church spoke the Word of God. Thus God clearly approved the building of palaces for Bishops and God wanted anyone who disagreed with His Church to be burnt at the stake. Meanwhile, the duty of the poor was to work hard, say nothing and produce the food that all of us need.

CHAPTER THREE
RELIGION, AND A BIT OF HISTORY

So, what of religion? A difficult and a dangerous subject that can raise passions in an audience; it can even inspire suicide bombers. A key word in religion is 'belief', and 'belief' carries with it an essence of woolliness. Were belief not woolly, it would be called knowledge. Now, if you claim to have 'belief', then you can be friends with all your community; if you claim to have 'knowledge', then all those around will look at you with suspicion. In the third and fourth centuries there was antagonism between the main-stream Christians, and those who claimed to 'know' — the Gnostics. Christian 'belief', good: Gnostic 'knowledge', bad; or so the story has come down to us.

That of which you have knowledge, must be true: that in which you have belief, might be true. For this is what the words mean.

Perhaps we begin to see the place of the Church. An individual has his 'belief' and can rest in confidence that 'knowledge' lies within the Church. With such a structure the Church must be nervous of any individual who claims to have knowledge.

So what of religion? Is it something that takes place inside a human mind — or is it something external that the human mind latches onto? Does it come out of a Church, or out of a book? Or is it just a feeling? Go into a house for the first time and many people get a feeling — a happy home — or a sad house? Many years ago I drove to the Battlefield of Culloden, but I found the atmosphere so oppressive I turned round and came away without stopping. I suspect this was not so much a hangover of battlefield deaths, more a residual effect from generations of people coming to be emotional about a battlefield. Again, when I first visited St Peter's in Rome — visually very impressive — but the feeling was of many people passing through — a bit like a railway station. Here, then, are examples of an external world making a mark on an internal mind. As an experiment, think for a moment of a section of an external world becoming organised, getting its stories fitted together and adding a bit of excitement here and there. Then think of this organised section of the external world making a mark on a mind. Is this a description of religion? If so, who was the organiser? Was it a Church, or was it God? Or both? Then the really uncomfortable question, 'Was it true?'

Belief is comparatively easy: but knowledge is a bit like handling a hedgehog — it needs to be done carefully,

> Did Jesus Christ exist? Yes, I believe so. Did He change water into wine? Wine is something known to change the state of the human mind.

Enthusiasm can of course push the language of belief into the language of knowledge. As Handel magnificently set it, 'I KNOW that my Redeemer liveth!'

But it is easier to relate the word 'know' to physical objects. (I know my way to the station.) A teaching may be a matter of belief, but a church you can know — with all its moss in the gutters and woodworm in the pews. 'Our statue of Mary is not impressive enough — we ought to buy a bigger one.' Perhaps the church with a small c is more important than we realised: it is a solid fact: something we can know: something we can work on: something to get our teeth into. Frequently you hear the words 'Our church'. Our church we know: God's church we believe in.

An Indian teacher told a story — a man wanted to be made better, so he set out to go to the hospital. He came to a crossroads. Now the hospital lay on the road to the right, and so long as the man turned right he would get to the hospital. If the man believed that the hospital was to the right, he would travel more easily.

This book has value only insofar as it triggers ideas in the mind of you, the reader. Although if we go back to the 'woodworm in the pews' order of reality, and if you have a table with one short leg then —. Belief, religion and knowledge are all things that happen inside a human mind, but do they have any existence outside?

'Belief', without a human believer does not seem to make any sense at all. How about religion? Religion has a great many very solid elements, starting with a church building and its woodworm, then there are holy days (sorry, holidays) and Christmas dinner. There are Parish boundaries, rules of acceptable behaviour, bishops sitting in Parliament and don't forget that libraries and hospitals both spring from religious roots. History books tell us of many wars that claim religion to be their justification. (Indeed, as I write, there is catastrophic war in Syria with a strong religious undercurrent.) Thus, whether we like it or not, whether we take part in it or not, none of us can avoid living in a world that has been significantly shaped by religion.

But then I hear you cry, 'Religion is about the spiritual world!' And it is here that I begin to have problems. My twentieth century upbringing makes me uncomfortable with any sort of parallel world in which magic plays a part, and I am unsure whether changing the word 'magic' into 'miracle' makes any difference. My local church requires me to say out loud that Jesus Christ "was crucified under Pontius Pilate; he suffered death and was buried. On the third day he rose again —." Other accounts suggest that He was placed on a shelf in a rock-cut tomb, rather than being buried, but let us not quibble about the detail. The important point is that He was dead, and came back to life. Something that our present-day scientific world is unable to explain. I get the feeling from today's churchgoers that miracles were real in the past, but for some reason we don't talk about, they stopped and they don't happen today. It is not a good explanation, but it is the best one we have! I am aware that there are shades of belief in this area. Anyone talking to a television camera after escaping from a car crash is likely to say, "It was a miracle!" And it is not difficult to imagine a whole range of meanings from the simple "I was lucky," through to the deeply religious, "God intervened on my behalf and overruled the laws of nature!"

If we go back five or six hundred years the world would seem to be a very different place. I believe the human mind itself had the same capacity then as now, but the range of ideas and everyday knowledge available to it were very different. You could gain religious credit watching the raising of The Host, or get a black mark by eating a pork chop on Friday. Your future could be foretold by reading the positions of the planets and you could get pains in your stomach if you fell out with the village witch. We may discount such things today as fanciful imaginings, but to the people involved, they were very real. We are getting close to saying that miracles can happen if you believe that they can happen: and so we come back to belief. I suggested a page or two ago that belief is something that happens inside the mind of a human believer. If you need a miracle, then work on your own mind! If praying to God helps, then so be it!

Looking at a broader meaning for the word 'religion', it has to be more than the occasional miracle; it has to be a story. For Christians the story comes from the Gospels in the New Testament, backed up by the letters of Paul and by the traditional tales told in the Old Testament. For Muslims the background is even clearer; Allah communicated directly with Mohammed, who wrote, or dictated, the Koran.

Not for the first time, we come up against the recurring problems of religion — transmission and interpretation. We tend to forget that for three-quarters of Christian existence, transmission was by a man on foot carrying a hand-written book. If he was lucky, he might have a donkey and a companion. Interpretation is even more of a problem. Most, if not all religious groups place high value on uniformity of belief and yet the history of religion, any religion, seems to tell tales of division. (But then, it is division that catches the attention of historians!) To try to hold things together, you need a far reaching authority — a church. To do its job, to encourage and spread a uniform belief, a church also has to have power to admonish any who stray from the approved path.

Once again, my attempts to discuss religion come back to 'belief', and if I am right, belief is something that goes on inside a human mind. However, there is one thing that has a very solid existence in the material world and that is the Church. As well as an obvious building and a graveyard, the Church has people, and books, and a network of communications; it teaches people how to behave and what to believe. Where belief is widespread and powerful, then the church is powerful. I feel I ought to say that God created a teaching, then men built a Church so that this teaching could spread to all mankind. But not everything went according to plan.

To start with, those people who put together our primary book of teaching, the Bible, chose to include a great quantity of traditional Jewish material, history and law books, along with the story of the creation of the world. No doubt this seemed very reasonable at the time, for Christianity was then regarded as no more than a minor variation on the Jewish faith. Indeed, Jesus was a Jew — wasn't he? There is no doubt that there is much interesting and valuable material in what we now call 'The Old Testament', but it did add complexity. There is so much written material that it is not difficult, with a bit of careful selection, to find words and phrases to support any view you wish to promote. As Antonio says in 'The Merchant of Venice', "The devil can cite scripture for his purpose."

Henry VIII had trouble with Leviticus 20:21, "And if a man shall take his brother's wife, it is an unclean thing; — they shall be childless." On the other hand, Deuteronomy 25:5 told him that if there are two brothers and one dies, the surviving brother should lie with the widow and their child become the heir to the dead brother. One really does wonder whether the Bible is the right place for this sort of debate.

Moving on to the New Testament and the Greek delight in theological argument, the essay on Constantine sets out another sort of complexity. But the practical task of the day was to found a Church that would link ideas of the spirit to the practicalities of everyday life. Thus, on the spiritual side, the Church had to study, understand and protect the teaching handed down to it, then ensure that the teaching was made available to all who wanted it. There were some for whom this was all they wanted, and they went off to live as hermits, or to found a monastery. But the word 'Church' as we usually understand it, requires a presence in the everyday community and here it has to face up to people whose ideas may not match its own. Its conviction in its own rightness leads the Church to try to convert others, to expand, to build and to take over. It begins to sound a bit like a supermarket! I suppose we should conclude that there is a weakness in the human frame that likes material success and the Church could not escape infection.

There is one feature of the Church that has had little mention so far: a feature that attracts many people. Warmth! Whether it be shelter for a tramp on a cold night; comfort for a bereaved parent, or Christmas dinner for the homeless with the Salvation Army. It may be a feeling of relief after confession, or just a sense of belonging — somewhere to go for help; somewhere to get involved. Being part of God's family is a strong glue for holding a community together.

Robert Browning wrote: -

"God's in his heaven,

All's right with the world."

A bit of Victorian romanticism, perhaps, but a splendid target to aim for: belief, put into practice, and leading to a better world. Both God and the government would approve.

If we just use Browning's line, "God's in his heaven" for a moment; drawing back the curtains on a lovely summer's morning, the line might come to the least religious of people, meaning happiness, contentment and appreciation of a beautiful world. The same line might bring a different person to his knees in fervent prayer. The same words can carry different messages, or different degrees of the same message. Central to all Christian thinking is Christ suffering on the Cross. Does this mean that He was enduring extreme pain: or does it mean that He was permitting the material processes of this world to proceed without divine intervention? Take care with words! Think of Moses speaking Hebrew; Christ speaking Aramaic and Paul, Greek, then all this squeezed into the Latin straitjacket before being translated into English. Then somebody stands up and claims the Bible is the word of God, and taps his King James Version.

"In the beginning was the Word," so begins the Gospel according to John, "and the Word was with God, and the Word was God." This powerful statement has focused the attention of Christians on the Word; the Word of God, and from there to the whole Bible as the Word of God. But is this what John meant? Some see 'The Word' as code for 'Jesus Christ' and thus demonstrating the central position of Jesus from the very beginning. Others might see a parallel with, 'The Teaching', as used by Buddhist monks.

My knowledge of Greek philosophy from the fourth century BC is sketchy, to say the least, but Socrates and Plato seem to talk of a 'non-visible realm of Forms' with which the eternal soul can have contact, and from which comes the shaping of an unstable visible world. It seems to me very likely that this was the concept that got condensed down into 'word'. In the beginning was the Form!

It certainly makes some sort of sense if we think of religion up in the realm of Forms, having to convert itself into the rough and ready world of words, before it can appear in the unstable visible world. It is also a useful reminder that some of the ideas that surface in Christianity have roots that go a long way back.

CHAPTER FOUR
THE BIBLE

"And the Lord spake unto Moses, saying, —" (Exodus 13:1)

So, there we have it: the words were the words of God, written down by Moses!

Well, — not quite. The writings that came together to make up the Bible have a complex history of their own. The Bible on my desk at the moment has, on its front cover, "Today's King James Version", words which immediately give me three reasons for thinking these are not the actual words of God as given to Moses. Moving on to open the cover, I see it was first published in 2002 ... about three thousand years too late! It is also written in English, a language unknown to Moses. OK, I know I'm being unreasonable, but I am just trying to emphasise the gap between what Moses, or anybody else, said or wrote in Biblical times, and what a Bible you might look at today, says they said.

Consideration of any ancient writing falls naturally into two parts. Firstly, who wrote it, and what meaning were they intending to convey? Secondly, by what route did this writing get to us? A copy off a copy off a copy of a translation of a copy is the sort of pattern we usually meet. There are clearly cases where an original document has survived into the present day; the 'Magna Carta' comes to mind. You can go along and look at it, and if you are clever enough, you can read it! But I don't think there is a single 'original document' that went into the making of the Bible: instead, there are (or were) countless books, scrolls, pages and fragments which have been studied and assessed, translated and compared by wise men: a process that goes back to the days when the inspirational teaching of the Prophets was changing over to a teaching based on Holy Scripture. When I first met this subject, it was called 'The Higher Criticism'.

If we think first of all of the Old Testament, we need to be aware that there was a group of students working within a school known as the Masoretes of Tiberias in the eighth, ninth and tenth centuries AD. This school was devoted to the preservation and accurate copying of Old Testament (i.e. Jewish) texts. Thus our prime source today for the Old Testament is the Masoretic Text. Another, rather better known text is the Septuagint, a translation of the Hebrew Bible into Greek made about 260BC in Alexandria. There are other, more recent discoveries, such as the Dead Sea Scrolls, but they have done little to shake the basic reliability of the Masoretic Text.

Looking for solid history in the Old Testament, we might reasonably start with the great ancestor, Abraham. Somewhere in the middle of the second millennium BC, he was told by The Lord to leave his home in Haran (probably Harran in Southern Turkey, near the Syrian border) and go to Canaan (now Israel), around five hundred miles away.

Now there is an inscription in the name of the Egyptian Pharaoh, Merneptah, of 1210 BC or thereabouts which gives us the name of 'Israel' for the first time. Rather depressingly, it says, "Israel is laid waste, its seed is no more!" Clearly Egyptian propaganda.

Trying to put a story together out of not very much evidence, I see a number of semi-nomadic groups circulating over a wide area and finally coming together in the hills of northern Palestine: one group bringing with it tales of slavery and an escape from Egypt. This gathering together would be about the tenth or ninth century BC and there is an inscription that records Omri as ruler/king of Israel at this sort of time. It is worth noting that the rainfall increases as you go north in this part of the world and northern Palestine is a better place to live than the dry south. But why live in the hills? It looks as though the lower lands towards the Mediterranean coast were already occupied by Philistines. The one thing that held these various tribes of Israel together was their worship of The One God, YHWH. Unfortunately, this was the very thing that brought them into conflict with all their neighbours, the Canaanites, the Philistines and the Amalekites of the Negev. Perhaps we should remember that the story of 'a land flowing with milk and honey' came from the estate agent's handout; reality was a world of squabbling with the neighbours, much the same as it is now, three thousand years later.

It may well be that the Canaanites, with their old-fashioned religion, had been the previous occupants of this land of Israel, and they were very reasonably upset by having their land allocated to somebody else by a God they didn't believe in! Very recent work is beginning to suggest that it was the Canaanites who invented the alphabet, and saved our children from cuneiform or hieroglyph.

The Israelites were looking forward to the time when God's rule would become universal and the Old Testament can be looked upon as a history written to encourage faith in YHWH.

The name of God requires a little explanation: firstly, the Hebrew language didn't bother much about vowels; secondly, the name of God was not supposed to be spoken; thus there were a number of substitute names: Adonai, Jehovah or, for academics, Tetragrammaton. I shall adopt the usual custom of adding a couple of vowels, so that you can read 'Yahweh', but don't say it out loud.

The first few hundred years saw Israel guided by the early Prophets, Hosea, Amos, Micah and the first Isaiah from the eighth century BC. Clearly this was religion taught by direct contact and word-of-mouth. As time went on, the worship of Yahweh divided into what we might think of as three flavours; the hot and ecstatic teaching direct from the Prophets (and, presumably, from those trained to carry on the work of the Prophets); then a calmer, more ordered, more legalistic style in the Royal Courts, and then, among the common people, a friendlier, more human religion. But Yahweh remained a fierce God and a hard taskmaster. Being God's Chosen People was not easy!

The very land on which they lived was given to them by God and thus the land, together with themselves and Yahweh, were bound together. Other material elements contained within their belief included the Divine manifestations granted to the Ancestors, Abraham and his family; together with the law-giving on Mount Sinai and the legend/memory of the Exodus.

I have never heard the subject discussed, but the Christian churches, both Catholic and Protestant, teach from the Old Testament as well as the New, so this fierce God Yahweh must still be with us. But I am reminded of the Cathar heretics of Southern France in the twelfth century who saw significant differences between the God of the Old Testament and the God of the New. But the Pope said they were wrong.

Around 722 BC the land of Israel came under attack from the Assyrians and the Israelites were squeezed out of Israel and down into the smaller and less hospitable land of Judah. Thus began a sequence of misfortunes for the Jewish Race that their excitable Prophets insisted were the result of a falling away from the proper worship of Yahweh.

If we now move on to the New Testament, you might be expecting an easier story, perhaps a scene a few months after the crucifixion where the Famous Four sit down to write their Gospels and record the world-shaking events of Jesus' ministry and teaching. Sorry — it wasn't quite like that. The names attached to the Gospels are traditional labels essential for reference purposes, but they disguise the fact that we have no idea who actually wrote them! Were they written whilst the events were still fresh in the mind? Well, no. Jesus was crucified in the year AD 30, plus or minus a year or two. Dating the four gospels is not an easy task: my understanding of current thinking by the experts puts the writing of Gospels called Matthew, Mark, Luke or John into the period from AD 65 to AD 120. That is from 35 to 90 years after the event! It may of course be that notes had been written down earlier, and the 65/120 dates were the dates of the writing up for circulation or publication. We don't know. Clearly a direct Disciple of Jesus was not writing in AD 120.

'The Word of God', as spelled out in the Bible, has long been central to Christian belief, and although some people were vaguely aware that the text had been translated from one language to another, this would have been done under 'divine guidance' a long time ago: so that was all right. The words they read were indeed 'The Word of God.'

From the fifth until the sixteenth century these 'Words' were the ones that came from the hand of Jerome. Jerome was the secretary to Pope Damasus I (366 – 384) and the Pope set him the task of reviewing the different Latin texts of the Bible then in circulation and producing a better version. In later life, Jerome retired to a monastery in Bethlehem where he produced a complete new Latin Bible, working from both Greek and Hebrew material. He finished this about the year AD 406. This was the Vulgate or common Bible, and was the Book that dominated the Christian world for more than a thousand years: the Council of Trent in 1546 declared it the 'authentic' Latin version of the Bible and required it to be used in all sermons, lectures and the like. (Not bad, at its eleven hundred and fortieth anniversary!) It is worth a marginal note that Jerome himself denied inspiration: this was his own crafted translation: it was not God's gift of a Latin text. However, this was soon forgotten and for most people the Vulgate became 'The Word of God.' Jerome was in many ways a strange man. He was strongly drawn to the ascetic life but clearly had a major struggle with his sexual urges. He was haunted by visions of dancing girls. He had a friend, a noble lady called Paula, who had a young daughter. Now imagine a middle-aged Jerome writing to this teenage girl explaining his problems with sex. He seemed to think this would help the girl in facing lifelong virginity!

Whilst dealing with marginal notes, give a thought to the way in which religious texts are studied and used. They are examined, re-examined, chewed over and disputed upon. Their deepest recesses are explored for possible allegorical or prophetic meanings. Gillian Evans, in her contribution to 'The Oxford Illustrated History of the Bible', puts it very neatly: -

> "No meaning which could be got out of scripture which was in keeping with orthodoxy could be thought of as an invention, since God would necessarily have thought of it first and placed it in the text ready to be found by the spiritually minded reader."

Now think of the translator faced with the task of fitting such a text into a different language. Not just the words: but a whole wealth of theological undercurrent! Surely only a sublime optimist could expect a translation to correctly interpret, preserve and transmit such a kaleidoscope of meanings. (Unless, of course, there was Divine Guidance.) I don't wish to appear cynical in this matter; but I do recommend caution.

Only a bishop can create a new bishop: thus the Church sees an unbroken chain stretching back from the present day, back from bishop to preceding bishop until the very first bishops were created by one of the Twelve Apostles. Thus there is a spiritual link from now, back into biblical times and there is personal contact with the love of Jesus Christ Himself. This 'Apostolic Succession', as the Church calls it, focuses attention on the Apostles and on how they tackled their task of spreading the knowledge and the love of Christ after He had Ascended. Rome has refined this idea so that they see the Apostle Peter becoming the first Pope, establishing an unbroken line of succession thereafter.

I may find myself in a very small minority here, but I don't think the Apostles make a terribly good showing in the New Testament. Particularly if we accept that the Four Gospels were written later, by somebody else. And if we remember that, strictly speaking, Paul was not an apostle. But then, in the wider world, an Apostle's task was to preach and to spread the Gospel by word of mouth so, perhaps, we should not expect carefully constructed historical records. It is not difficult to imagine a new colony of Christians, surrounded by unsympathetic neighbours, working to set down in writing their own group's 'creation myth': how they were visited and inspired by an Apostle who later went on to be martyred. (And nothing makes a story stick in the mind like a really messy death!) Of the Twelve Apostles, it looks as though only one died of old age (John).

The shortest story is that of Judas Iscariot who, shortly after the Crucifixion, committed suicide, probably by hanging himself. The interesting point here is that Matthias was rapidly elected to fill the space, suggesting that the number 'twelve' was important, and had to be restored, but for what reason we do not know. James, son of Zebedee seems never to have left the area of Jerusalem and was caught up in the persecutions of Herod Agrippa and was beheaded in AD 44. However, putting that on one side, he is also said to have preached the Gospel in Spain, then after his beheading (in Jerusalem?) his body (plus head?) was taken to Spain and buried at Santiago de Compostela which became a great centre for pilgrims, tourists and traders which flourishes to this day. Confusing stories abound. Bartholomew went on a mission to the East, perhaps Mesopotamia, perhaps Ethiopia or even India: he was martyred in Armenia by being beaten and executed or, alternatively, beheaded, perhaps after being flayed alive: or, again, the flaying alive followed by being crucified head downwards. One of his arms is said to survive in Canterbury Cathedral. For an obvious, but not very nice reason, he was made the Patron Saint of tanners! One story in which I have slightly more confidence is that of Doubting Thomas who set up a successful ministry in Southern India.

All these tales were no doubt created and circulated to keep people talking about Christianity at a time when persecution was common and widespread. There may also have been an attempt to change the attitude that saw Christianity as no more than a minor variation on the Jewish Religion; and change it into a more distinctive view of Christianity as something new and different and based on personal sacrifice.

One Apostle who has not been mentioned so far is Peter, the first Pope and keystone of the Roman Catholic Church. He is the only one for whom there is any surviving material evidence. (I discount the various bits of Apostles bought by Cathedrals and Monasteries from passing monks in the twelfth century.) It is clear that Peter came to Rome and although we know practically nothing about the last twenty years of his life, he was crucified (upside down, according to legend) during the persecutions of Nero around AD 64 – 68. Seen as a criminal by the authorities, no official arrangements would have been made for his burial. It seems that his followers had a rather clever idea and buried Peter's body in an already existing grave on the slope of the Vatican Hill near to Nero's arena (and presumably near to the site of his crucifixion). Secrecy was essential. Somewhere between the years 150 and 200, a fairly anonymous altar or shrine was set up to mark the grave, to be followed not long after by a small group of rooms, centred on the altar and fitted between the pre-existing Roman tombs. (Known today as the Red Wall complex, it could be described as the world's very first Christian church.) As time went on, the red wall adjacent to the altar developed a crack and a fairly rough wall was built in front of the crack to prevent further movement. I feel the urge to say at this point, "This is where the story really begins!" For in a concealed chamber, inside this rough support wall, were found the bones of Saint Peter! Their discovery was announced by Pope Paul VI in 1968. The acknowledged grave of Peter was below the altar structure — so how had the bones moved upwards into a cavity inside this later wall? We can only suppose there was some time of crisis, with a fear that the bones would be dug up and destroyed. Among the sacred bones were found the bones of a mouse — obviously a late arrival on the scene — and I am pleased to note that after Peter's bones had been cleaned, identified and recorded, they were put into plastic boxes and replaced in the cavity in which they had been found — together with a plastic box containing the bones of the mouse!

Next time you are in St Peter's Basilica in Rome, look at the great altar and think of Saint Peter's bones, and of all those early structures that survived both the construction of the first basilica by

Constantine in the 330's, and the rebuilding in the sixteenth century, and which still exist in the ground underneath.

Saint Peter's Basilica, Rome
The screen behind which lie the bones of Saint Peter

It may have been some growth in the human spirit of enquiry: it may have been increasing frustration at the dictatorship of the Roman church: but by the end of the fifteenth century, scholars were looking afresh at religious writings. It was noticed that there were old texts lying forgotten in libraries that were not quite the same as the Vulgate. Generally speaking, they were not wildly different; but the fact that there were any differences at all was enough to cut the ground from under the feet of those who sought "The Very Word of God". It was noticed that some texts were in Latin and some were in Greek and scholars were aware that the written language of the Biblical lands was Greek. (They may have spoken Aramaic, or Syriac, but those who could write, used Greek.) Thus, around 1500, it became clear to scholars that as the Old Testament had originally been written in Hebrew, and the New Testament had been written in Greek, therefore the surviving texts in those languages were likely to be more reliable than Jerome's fifth century translation into Latin.

It was in 1516 that Erasmus of Rotterdam published the first of these studies: a bilingual version of the New Testament. On the right-hand side of each page was the familiar Vulgate text in Latin, whilst on the left was the comparable text in Greek.

CHAPTER FIVE
THE CHURCH

If we go back to the Council of Constantinople in 381, when the Emperor Theodosius set Christianity in concrete, (refer to the chapter on Constantine for a bit more detail of this event) and if we then think forward to the years in the second half of the fourteenth century, when most of Europe was reshaping itself after the loss of a third of the population to the Black Death around 1349: then we have, almost exactly, a thousand years of what we might think of as Rome's heyday. The very first moves may have happened in the Greek world, but the centre of power very rapidly moved west, to Rome. Rome was in control: at least, that's how Rome saw it. Rome was the centre of the known world: all roads lead there. Churches in Byzantium, or the Coptic, or the Syriac varieties of Christianity hardly existed so far as Rome was concerned. Indeed, later, when pleas came from Constantinople for help in defending themselves against the invading Muslims, Rome turned a deaf ear. After all, Muslims were less of a threat to Roman theology than the diabolically deviant Christians of Byzantium!

As usual, there are two ways of looking at the situation. On the one hand, the Church was sternly disciplinarian, with its one book, The Vulgate, and its one Pope, a descendant from Saint Peter, the holder of the keys to heaven. All distracting subjects were suppressed, no science, no drama, no study of the natural world; and art was permissible only if it was used to enhance religious teaching. All of life was to be devoted to God, according to the Roman rules. Does Jesus Christ have one nature or two — give the wrong answer and your life could be in danger. As time moves onward, language itself becomes a weapon of the Church. You were supposed to lead your life according to the teachings in the Bible — but the Bible was in Latin! You could, of course, go to your local priest, who would tell you what the Bible said — or what he thought it said — or what he thought you ought to hear!

I am sure that good Catholics saw things very differently. They must have thought back to the routine persecutions of the days

THE CHURCH

before Constantine; followed by the bitter conflict between different Christian ideas and the constant warfare, both spiritual and physical, against a multitude of heretics. The Council of Constantinople must have come as a blessed relief: at last, all Christians were singing from the same hymn sheet! And so it was to be for the next thousand years. The whole of Western Europe, with its multitude of races, of languages and of customs, came together every Sunday to worship with the Latin Mass. Why would anyone want to disrupt such an excellent system? Warfare still went on, of course, but it was easier to understand your enemy, and it was only later that people started to look back on those thousand years as the 'Dark Ages'.

Then, ever so slowly, the log jam began to creak. Two ideas were stirring. Firstly, why had the Church got so much money? And secondly, if the Bible was so important, why were people not allowed to read it for themselves? The first point led on to a comparison between the very simple, down to earth life as portrayed in the Bible, and the grand existence and splendid buildings that the Church now saw as appropriate to its position. On the second point, there were a number of early attempts to translate the Bible into a language ordinary people could read, starting with John Wycliff in 1383: the chapter on Henry VIII tells something of the Power that rose up to put a stop to that.

So, when we are re-designing the history course for our schools, how about — "The Reformation grew out of seeds planted by the Black Death — discuss!"

It is important to note that during 'The Thousand Years' religious study was the work of monks and priests, with their material restricted to the Vulgate Bible and related books. (Perhaps there were nuns as well, but we hear very little about them. Every nun had a male confessor who would require any writing that showed originality, to be burnt.) Christianity was the Roman church! To deviate from Roman rules was to risk a hot death! To us in the twenty-first century this will sound like dictatorship at its most brutal, but I suggest that to a peasant in the fourteenth or fifteenth centuries (peasants being 95% of the population) the Church offered certainty and security in a very unsure world. Had they thought about it at all, I am sure that the peasants would have fought against any attempt to unseat the Catholic Church, for in the Church lay their security and the hope of a future life in heaven. We can begin to see the problems facing those scholars with new ideas; the men carrying the seeds of Reformation. Not only was the Church against them, but also a population that had been thoroughly taught by the Church. The path to Reformation was not easy, and it was led by brave men! What was it that drove them onward? I can think of only one name: God! Sorry, Catholics, but it was clearly time for a change.

Much emotional stuff is written around the Reformation, but let's have a go at a calmer view. In the earliest days, new Christian communities would have kept close together out of a sense of self-preservation. Worshipping together, their beliefs and rituals would have become standardised within their group. And if we then think of groups of this sort, widely scattered, with pagans in between, then it is not difficult to imagine one of these Christian groups adopting a slightly different form of ritual, or perhaps, following a particularly charismatic leader. This gives us a picture of Christianity before AD 300. There was always tension in the air, with the risk of exposure to pagan authorities, and perhaps a sense of rivalry and competition with other Christian groups. Remember also, that Greek was a language well-suited to theological nit-picking, something that Latin speakers were unable to understand. One fairly straightforward difference of opinion grew to near 'World War' proportions. "Jesus Christ was the Son of God, born of the Virgin Mary" — seems a fairly obvious statement for any Christian, and is well supported by the Bible. BUT: we are Christians: our faith and our name depend upon the person of Jesus Christ. We cannot tolerate a world before the Annunciation without a Jesus Christ!! Guess which side won? You are probably wrong! The side that followed the Bible, lost! (The chapter on Constantine has much to say about these matters.)

THE CHURCH

The point for us to understand today, is that early Christianity was not a world of sweetness and light: there was much disagreement and conflict. Whilst in parallel, the non-religious world was in a state of some confusion as well, with the central authority of Roman Government losing its grip, and the surrounding tribes building up rival organisations with political and military abilities. Into this world of political and religious uncertainty came Constantine.

I think it came as a shock to early Christians when they realised that devotion to God and His Son Jesus Christ was not enough! Unwavering faith and loving your neighbour was still not enough! They needed organisation! They needed Bishop Leaders to guide them and to speak on their behalf. (No doubt these Bishops took on a social standing with perhaps a house and an income to suit.) Almost without noticing it, the Church was drifting into the shape of a political party. The one thing a political party needs to do is to stick together: we all need to believe in the same things! Thus, hunting down heretics became a first task of the Christian Party, "Love your neighbour as yourself," unless, of course, you think he is a heretic!

It is important to remember in any study of early history that we are totally dependent upon what the people of the time chose to record. And, in the most general terms, they recorded what they saw as unusual. Keeping this idea firmly at the back of our minds — the raging topic of the fourth and fifth centuries (some might add the sixth and the seventh as well) was heresy. Perhaps the oldest of the heresies was Gnosticism, a view of life that saw God in a spiritual world upstairs, whilst down here, the solid world around us was the work of an evil creator. The specifically Christian heresies mostly centred on the relationship between God and Jesus, and here there was endless variety. Jesus had to be human in order to suffer on the Cross and thus save mankind: on the other hand, he was the Son of God and therefore divine (and, of course, could feel no pain). Were there two Jesus's: or was there one Jesus with two natures? Debates of this sort went on endlessly and unless you were prepared to adjust your belief to suit the currently favoured view, you ran the risk of being discarded as a heretic. Christianity had started off with open arms; welcoming all comers; but was beginning to show signs of becoming an exclusive club. Bishops were increasing in their power and authority, and were probably not slow to use the changing patterns of heresy to further their own image and career.

The civilised world was falling apart with all this Christian bickering. Something had to be done! So in 325 Constantine called all the bishops together to a meeting at his palace in Nicaea. As mentioned in the chapter on Constantine, some degree of success was achieved and the Creed as set out at Nicaea still has a place in present day church services. But Nicaea left too many loopholes: too many places where rival ideas could creep in. So a second Council was called by the Emperor Theodosius at Constantinople in 381, to tighten things up. But controversy kept raging: partly over the nature of Jesus Christ, and partly over the relative ambitions of Alexandria and Constantinople with the occasional outburst from Rome and from Antioch.

Nestorius, the Bishop of Constantinople, had been accused of being a heretic by Cyril, the Bishop of Alexandria, so Nestorius persuaded the Emperor Theodosius II to set up a Council which came to be called The Third Ecumenical Council, held at Ephesus in 431. There was much skulduggery: the opening of the Council is well described by a quote in Charles Freeman's book, 'A.D. 381':-

> "Cyril and his supporting bishops arrived early" (or, to put it another way, they started the meeting before their opponents had arrived) "and bullied their way to success, not least through bribery of Theodosius' court; this was so extensive that Cyril's own clergy in Alexandria complained their diocese had been reduced to poverty."

Nestorius was condemned and he retreated to Antioch.

THE CHURCH

These occasional Church Councils were awarded the name 'Ecumenical' with the sense that they carried the full authority of the whole Church. They continue up to recent times with the Second Vatican Council of 1962 being numbered 21. They provide a valuable resource for historians because much of the discussion and the decisions made were written down and stored away. Indeed, I was once told that Nicaea was the very first meeting for which a full set of minutes is still available.

There was a Council held at Ephesus in 449, which did not make it onto the list of Ecumenicals, and therefore does not have a number. They agreed that Christ had one single nature but it seems to have been a rowdy gathering with cries of "Cyril is immortal!" and "Nestorius should be burnt!" Later, all those who had attended were excommunicated by Pope Leo.

The Fourth Ecumenical Council was held in Chalcedon in 451, and its first task was to 'set aside' the 449 Council. The everlasting debate on the nature of Jesus Christ went on — and on.

> "Our Lord Jesus Christ, the same perfect in Godhead and also perfect in manhood; truly God and truly man, —."

However, the Coptic Churches and the Syrian Church of the East did not like this splitting of Jesus into two parts, so they went their own way, separating themselves from the Graeco-Roman Church; a separation which lasted until Pope John Paul II (now Saint John Paul) brought them back together in 1984, declaring the differences to be little more than terminology.

Clearly, these Ecumenical Councils had their uses: their records included lists of 'canons' or instructions on how the church was to manage its business; what was permitted and what was not. But there was a bit of a problem with the 'theology' of these meetings which suggested that since all bishops were working under Divine Guidance, then all decisions would be unanimous. But it clearly didn't happen quite like that — at least as far as the popular reports tell us. There was much mud-slinging, name-calling and generally rather childish behaviour. And yet — although the records were not physically changed —; the understanding of them underwent — what shall we say — a bit of adjustment. The participants acquired a rather more respectable image and some even came to be looked upon as among the Church Fathers. (That powerful group whose membership was never defined.) Perhaps the move to Rome and the change of language helped. Respect reached a high point around the year 600 when Pope Gregory the Great equated the four Councils of Nicaea, Constantinople, Ephesus and Chalcedon, along with the Four Gospels, as the cornerstones of Christian orthodoxy.

The Latin speaking Christian World of Rome in AD 600 was very different from the Greek speaking Christian World, just released from official persecution, shortly after the year 300. And I don't think the usual history books offer an adequate explanation. So, let us try adding two and two together, and see if we can do better than three and a half. We have to start by acknowledging a hole in our information. I have been unable to find dates or description for the move of Church Power and Authority away from the Greek world and into Rome. But it clearly happened.

Think, for a moment, of the Christians before their time of release. They must have been a people of strong and independent thought; determined to follow their own beliefs, whatever they were told by the pagan authorities; people we might describe today as 'bloody-minded'. Come the day of release; think of animals released from a pen, dashing off in all (theological) directions and snapping at anyone who got in their way. There is a turn of phrase used to describe a situation where rational organisation has zero chance of success: 'it is like herding cats!' I think that the Christian leaders, through much of the fourth century, were trying to herd cats. There is, of course, no mention of cats in the records, but there is a great deal about heresy!

There were Gnostics and there were Arians. In my view, the Arians were by far the largest group of Christians at the time, but their society was illiterate and so has left us no records. There were Priscillians; followers of the first Christian bishop to be executed, and then there were the varieties of opinion, Adoptionism, Donatism, Macedonianism, Manichaeism, Marcionites, Monothelitism, Nestorianism, Novatianism, Pelegianism and Sabellianism. This is beginning to look like a song by Tom Lehrer, so I shall stop — but there were a lot of them! Imagine the task of Senior Church Organisers faced with the problem of drawing all this together into one single, coherent Church. I think they could see only one solution — strong discipline — backed up by even more discipline. Torture was routinely used by Church Authorities to extract information or confession from those believed to have links with heretical groups. The only question worthy of debate was whether a senior churchman should, or should not, be present at the torture sessions. Any writing that disagreed with the approved teaching was to be burnt, and a law of 409 stated that any person failing to bring heretical writings to the bonfire could suffer the death penalty. These were hard times, and hard times require hard decisions.

It is worth giving a little more thought to the Priscillians with their leader and inspiration, Bishop Priscillian of Avila. (Active in Spain, with a concentration toward the north-west of that country.) In the 380's Church thinking was being pushed forward by Bishop Ambrose of Milan and by Bishop Augustine of Hippo. (Both of whom had dabbled in 'heretical' ideas earlier in their lives.) Ambrose seems to have been primarily concerned with achieving political power for the Church, while both of them seem to have had suspicions about Priscillian. They saw him as being too interested in spiritual matters and mysticism — not a team player — at least, not in their team. He was accused of being involved in the Manichaean heresy, (a return to a simple dualist world of good and evil where a Manichee was expected to pick out the gems of good from the mud of evil). Mani, the leader of this heresy, was a Persian, and Persia (now Iran) has always been regarded by the West with deep suspicion. Although it requires a certain amount of reading between the lines, I get the impression that part of the problem with Priscillian was his insistence on clerical celibacy at a time before Rome had made up its mind on this matter. Indeed, there is a suggestion that some senior church leaders not only slept with their wives, but they also felt free to sleep with any other female members of their household if they chose. The resulting children were becoming a bit of an embarrassment. It looks as though there were a number of reasons by Bishop Priscillian did not fit — he had to go!

The late fourth century was a time of much instability within both the religious world and the political world, with a lot of jockeying for position, and out of this confusion came an Imperial order condemning Priscillian and some of his associates. He was beheaded at Trier in 385 (Trier in Germany, near the border with Luxemburg). The charge was sorcery, and it illustrates the great fear of witchcraft that ran through the whole of society at this time, no matter how strong their Christian beliefs may have been. There were also people around with an eye on the property that was being confiscated. Meanwhile, back in Spain, Priscillian's followers survived for a while but came under increasing pressure from an antagonistic Church. For example, the Church issued an order allowing slaves in Priscillian households to leave their owners. So here we are; our history books tell us about Constantine and his efforts to get the Christian Church up and running, whilst later the same century (in Spain at least), torture chambers were in use to track down anyone who saw Christianity in a slightly different light. And slavery seems to have been so common that it only gets a mention by chance.

Even in my lifetime, the Catholic Church in Spain has seemed to be more severe than elsewhere.

Remembering that Priscillian and his followers had their primary centre of influence in north-west Spain, and noting the great church of that area, at Compostela — then reading of a fairly recent discovery that this church was built over a substantial number of closely packed Christian graves of the fourth and fifth centuries —

could it be that Priscillian's body was brought back from Trier to Compostela and that many of his followers chose to be buried close to his holy grave? Four hundred years later, in the ninth century, the Church established a shrine to St James at Compostela, presumably to focus attention on a 'main line' saint rather than on one they would prefer to forget. The Church was successful insofar as they established the most popular pilgrim's route in Europe from the ninth to the twenty-first century. Welcome to Sanpriscillian de Compostela!

Perhaps the greatest tragedy in the fourth century was the decision that any writing that did not promote main-line Christian thought was a waste of effort and a distraction. Any scholar suspected of being in any way heretical had his library burnt, and the works of Plato and Aristotle, if not burnt, were abandoned to rot away. Discarded in the same way was the great store of Greek drama, with its clear understanding of how human society worked, and its shrewd and often humorous assessment of political government. All gone: save by chance a small handful of surviving fragments.

Fortunately, Rome did not have control over the whole world, and some of these writings went East, where they were later picked up by Muslim scholars, translated into Arabic and stored in libraries. Although one feels they didn't deserve it, the Christians recovered some of this Greek/Arabic material as they drove the Muslims out of Spain in the twelfth and thirteenth centuries.

By the time of Gregory the Great, Pope from 590 to 604, (the man who dispatched Augustine to Britain to mop up a little local difficulty — see the chapter on Augustine) most of the Western World had been tidied up and squeezed into the tight-fitting suit that came to be known as Roman Catholicism.

Fourteen hundred years further on, it is easy for us to be critical: to condemn the raging intolerance; but then we have forgotten about the cats of heresy. If you were to see your life as a great long period of happiness (post death), then the short period of struggle (pre death) was easy to bear. It would even make a sort of sense were someone to be burnt at the stake 'for the good of their soul!' But our only knowledge of 'post death' is that given us by the Church and it is easy to see that without the Church, we are nothing (or would become nothing!). By AD 600 there was a degree of unity across Europe: a unity of thinking and, to some extent, a unity of behaviour and values. Christianity had created a larger community — surely a part of its intention! In order to focus the communal mind on this unity in Church, it had been necessary to obliterate some of the distractions; the fun of Greek drama; the serious mental exercises of the Greek philosophers and the natural human curiosity about the physical world around them.

Was the Church right or wrong in taking human beings along this path? I have no enthusiasm for the 'what if' school of historical speculation, but if the Roman Catholic Church had not laid a heavy hand on the reins guiding humanity in the fifth and sixth centuries, then it is easy to imagine a multitude of 'heresies' having their day, flourishing for a while, and then fading away, taking Christianity with them. On the other hand, I feel a little more certain that the seeds of Reformation were planted into the system from the very start. The inventive and the enquiring mind of man would not be held in check for all time.

There also seems to be a second, and very different story that runs through the last two thousand years; but a story that appears strangely lacking in deliberate control or direction. It seems to worship the same God, but has little or no connection with the organisation we know as 'The Church'. It looks something like this:
-

Crucifixion was a fairly common form of execution in the Roman world, but the Crucifixion of Jesus was seen to make a connection between gruesome death and spiritual achievement. Indeed, the pain suffered by Jesus on the Cross is shown to be an essential factor in the salvation of mankind, as we are reminded in Church to this day. The more enthusiastic of early Christians took, as their objective, to get close to Jesus — and Jesus was dead.

Therefore, to get yourself killed, preferably in some public and spectacularly gruesome way, was the high speed ticket to a place beside Jesus. It may have been true that these people saw the end of this world, and the coming of God's Kingdom, as very close: if not this year, then certainly by the next! So they would not be missing much by leaving life early; and they would get a good place in the queue at Heaven's Gate. My cynical side is beginning to show through, but we ought to remember that stories of blood and violence have always attracted readers, and the stories of how the martyrs faced death were popular reading from the fourth century onward, and if the victim was a pretty girl, then so much the better! (Think of a Catherine wheel.)

The very early years of Christianity have a clear focus on martyrs: those who have 'died in Christ'. Long before there were churches, Christians would meet at the burial site of a martyr. (Indeed, in some ways, we still do! We have put up a roof over the tomb and given the building the name of a saint, and we now call the tomb an altar, but the similarity is close.) Time went on and it began to sink in that God's Kingdom was not 'just around the corner'. (For those at a high spiritual level, it might be: but for the great majority, just about to go out and buy bread for the kid's tea — it wasn't!) So enthusiasm for martyrdom faded away. Where now?

The idea of martyrdom was still in the air, but actual death no longer seemed to be appropriate. So let us try taking all the elements of comfort and pleasure out of human life so that the task of getting closer to God can proceed unhindered! Among the first to follow this new 'ascetic' path was Antony, who went out to live alone in the Egyptian desert around the year 285. (See the essay on Augustine.) Two problems were quick to arise: firstly, others soon chose to follow Antony's example and perhaps damaged his idea of isolation; secondly, these desert hermits acquired a reputation as 'holy men' and attracted visitors. Some may have come for genuine spiritual guidance, but some will have come simply to admire the latest craze. And then, horror of horrors, some visitors were women!

So far in this book I have avoided special mention of women (for in this modern world we are all equal — aren't we?) But in ancient times things were very different. A woman was simply unable to reach the levels of spiritual and intellectual understanding achievable by men and it was probably best if she didn't even try. The woman's proper place was to bear and raise children — preferably male children, to carry forward the family and its interests. But women were the carriers of a serious problem; a problem that so often deflected men from their proper task. Let us be clear about this; we are told that a man sitting in a cave in the desert studying scripture would often be distracted by inappropriate thoughts. This affliction was clearly caused by women: they are the problem! The Good Book gives us the start of the story; Adam and Eve led an idyllic life in happiness and in close communion with God. Then Eve was led astray and persuaded Adam to join her in eating the fruit of the tree of the knowledge of good and evil (Genesis 2:17 – 3:6). "And the Lord God said unto the woman, 'What is this that thou hast done?'" (Genesis 3:13). Thus, in a stroke, Adam and Eve had lost the Garden of Eden, they had lost eternal life and they had lost their close association with God — all because of Eve (or, as the Church sometimes looked at the problem, because of the whole battalion of women, led by Eve. We could try a conversion into modern language and say SEX!) From the days of the Garden of Eden, the Christian Church has seen sex, at best, as a rival, and at worst, as an enemy!

So, there is a fundamental problem built into Church Authority; we don't like sex; we see it as a powerful competitor for the minds of men. (We also have an uncomfortable feeling that it might be stronger than we are, but never admit it.) We would really like to abolish it altogether, but even Churchmen could see a problem in going down that path. So, praise for the celibate priest and praise for the committed virgin!

But the problem refuses to go away. It is essential Christian thinking that Christ was a human being (at least in part). This meant that He had to be born — and before that — yes, I remember, there was an angel! The Church has battled with itself over the centuries to get a human Jesus into this world without any mention of the forbidden word. From an Immaculate Conception of Mary to a visit from an angel, on through childbirth and out the other side as a virgin. Her perpetual virginity was confirmed by the Lateran Council of 649, and her Immaculate Conception (meaning that original sin had never entered her soul) was confirmed by the Catholic Church in 1854. The Church went on to assert, in 1950, that her body had been physically transported to Heaven and so efforts to find her grave should stop. I am trying to avoid phrases like, "gynaecology by majority vote in a men-only committee", but there is a serious point to be made.

Sex and religious belief are perhaps the most powerful driving forces behind both men and women, once they have access to adequate food and shelter. And these two forces are very, very different when seen through Christian eyes. My knowledge of the Hindu religion is very basic, but they clearly organise things differently; sex and religion seem to run along side by side with full-breasted goddesses carved into the stonework. But for the Christian Church things were difficult. We don't like it; we wish it would go away; but we can't run the world without it! Thus the Thousand Years of the Tight-Fitting Suit can be seen as a valiant attempt to construct and run a world with the absolute minimum influence or mention of sex!

I am sorry, I was distracted by women — back to the ascetic life! There is some detail about the growth of the monastic movement in the chapter on Augustine, but I think a quick sketch might be useful here.

Reading the New Testament, it is easy to get a picture of Jesus as a fairly ordinary sort of a man, leading a normal sort of life among an ordinary sort of community. (OK, I know there were some extraordinary moments, but the overall picture is one of domestic normality.) We may read of Jesus going off into the wilderness or the desert, but this seems to be no more than setting the scene for His encounter with the devil: it does not look to me as though Jesus was taking steps towards an ascetic life. The point I am trying to offer for consideration is that the Christian Church based itself upon the Jesus of the 'domestic normality' background. Not a great surprise, really; the people the Church was trying to teach would have come from that sort of background themselves. So where did this ascetic idea come from? I suspect it might be Christians taking over from a pre-existing custom. As Abba Moses, one of the Desert Fathers wrote, "Sit in thy cell and thy cell will teach thee all." Anyway, the ascetic life was a hard life with discipline as the key word — hard work, hard study and no comfort! At first there were men like Antony looking for isolation as a hermit; later, groups of like-minded people set up together to form monasteries, but still with the emphasis on discipline.

There seems to have been something of an avalanche in this style of living, for Athanasius wrote that "The desert has become a city", and the ascetic life spread from Egypt and up into Syria, where Simeon Stylites (390 – 459) tried to separate himself from the pilgrims and the sightseers by living on a small platform on top of a column — then his visitors brought ladders! One can understand the urge to get away and live alone, to study and to get closer to God. One can also understand the visitors' wish to satisfy their curiosity and perhaps add to their store of spiritual credits. But it is more difficult to come to terms with the element of showmanship that seemed to creep in and led Simeon to higher and higher columns and persuaded others to follow a similar path. I have recently seen (on the telly) Hindu holy men who also seemed to combine a contemplative and ascetic life with a fair dose of showmanship while dressed in a thin coating of wood ash. (If you rely on visitors to bring you food, then you have to do something to ensure they keep coming.) What I think we might be seeing in this move to asceticism is an underlying thought that finds great virtue in a man after all the material comforts and pleasures have been stripped away. Christians see it as an access to God. It seems to have started in Egypt and expanded through the third, fourth and fifth centuries. Then, out of nowhere, there appears a primitive monastic community on the west coast of Ireland. If my thinking is in any way correct, then this fifth century community would have looked to Authority in Alexandria and not to Rome at all. They were an early branch of a belief system that grew to become what we now know as the Coptic Church.

Rumours clearly reached Pope Celestine and started whatever is the papal equivalent of panic. Here was a rival organisation setting up in 'his' Europe. It may have been a small place and a long way away, but something had to be done! So around 430, he sent Palladius off to sort things out!

The meeting of Rome-based Palladius with the men from Egypt seeking isolation in Ireland has to be imagined. We learn later that there were differences on how to fix the date of Easter, and on the style of monastic haircut: one wonders if there were other, more interesting differences that got lost in the wastepaper baskets of Rome. This matter of a date for Easter has always caused a bit of a problem. Without wishing to become astronomically involved, a date which fixes fairly easily according to a lunar calendar encounters difficulties when it is transposed into the solar calendar that we all use. Indeed, the World Council of Churches was looking for a simpler solution as recently as 1997. As is well known, this Irish monastic movement expanded across Ireland, set up in Iona under Columba in 563 and eventually reached Lindisfarne in 635, inspiring other monastic settlements along the way. The 205 years from the west coast of Ireland to the east coast of England suggests a steady but slow progress.

So, for a couple of hundred years, three quarters of the British Isles (those parts not being invaded by Saxons, Danes or other pagans) followed a form of Christianity with roots in Egypt: a style of Christianity that formally separated itself from Rome at the Fourth Ecumenical Council at Chalcedon in 451. Arguments over the style of a haircut, or the method to be used in getting from a lunar date to a solar date seem pretty trivial to us, but for an expanding Roman Church they were a distasteful reminder that their brand of Christianity was not the first to arrive in the far west.

It is perhaps useful to look upon early Christianity in Britain as having three strands. Firstly, the obvious one, coming direct from Rome first with Germain, and much later with Augustine. Secondly (if I am right) from the hot sands of Egypt by way of Ireland. And thirdly, we should not forget that there were Christians in Britain during the Roman occupation (British bishops went off to a Council in Arles in 314). Whether this Christian presence survived the Roman departure, we don't know. If it did, it probably joined up with the Christianity of Irish flavour.

It is not difficult to imagine the Popes of the day having a vision of European unity under the Roman banner: Celestine sending Palladius to Ireland and Germain to Britain around 430, then Gregory sending Augustine to Britain in 596. (Sent in 596, arrived in 597!) The winds were blowing in Rome's favour, but not very fast. It was not until 664 at the Synod of Whitby that a formal decision was taken to follow the Roman path, rather than the Irish/Celtic one. (In passing, it is pleasant to see a major Church decision being made by a committee under the chairmanship of a woman: the Abbess Hilda.) And still another fifty-two years were to pass before Iona finally "submitted to Rome"! Then in 927 the various kings of England and the North drew together under Athelstan with an undertaking to suppress idolatry, and for the first time, England became one united kingdom: a Christian country that looked towards Rome.

CONSTANTINE

Towards the end of the third century the Roman Empire was huge and the neighbours were becoming ever more aggressive. In an attempt to get better control over armies operating many hundreds of miles away from Rome, Diocletian split the Empire into two halves, each half having an emperor (Augustus) and an assistant emperor (Caesar). A good idea, but not a success. It ended up with two contestants fighting for military control, Constantine and Maxentius. At the famous battle of Milvian Bridge in 312, Constantine had the vision of a Christian Cross in the sky, so he had his soldiers paint a cross on their shields: and went on to win. Constantine and his co-emperor Licinius set up a policy of religious toleration allowing Christians freedom to worship as they wished, all formalised as the Edict of Milan in 313. (It should be remembered that Christians had suffered fairly recent bouts of official persecution in 250, 258, 303 and, no, doubt, other times as well.)

Head of the Emperor Constantine (307-337) on public display in Rome

ESSAY - CONSTANTINE

In 324 Constantine managed to get rid of Licinius and take overall control. He moved the capital from Rome to Byzantium and re-named it Constantinople. The language of government drifted from Latin to Greek but, confusingly, the inhabitants of this new capital still referred to themselves as Romans (Romaioi in Greek). Constantinople was up and running and formally consecrated in the year 330 and was seen by many as a fortunate escape from the roughness of Rome with all its ancient and pagan overtones and traditions.

Constantine is a well-known name even today and he must be listed among the most effective emperors the world has ever seen. He seems to have sensed the rising of military organisation among the Germanic tribes and got out of the way, moving to the rather more stable Greek world with its access to the food supplies of Syria and Egypt. As a shrewd governor, he would be well aware of the growing power of Christian thought among the Greek-speaking peoples. He would also be aware that Christians did not speak with a single voice. There were a multitude of variations on Christian theology and each group seemed to be at war with all the others, throwing charges of heresy in all directions. Most of these points of contention would seem rather silly to us in the twenty-first century, but in the fourth, they were desperately important. Did Christ have one nature or two? When God put some of His substance into Jesus, did God become less? Had Jesus existed from the beginning of time before being made man?

Although Constantine is often referred to as the 'First Christian Emperor' this may not be entirely true (and perhaps not true at all). Such evidence as we have suggests that he was a follower of Sol Invictus, the unconquerable sun. (Could this be the reason we still go to church on the Day of the Sun?) Certainly Eusebius reports that Constantine decreed that the military regiments should recite their prayers to God every Sunday. However, it is important to note that much of our information on Constantine comes from a biography written by Eusebius, Bishop of Caesarea, and that his writing positively fizzes with enthusiasm for Christianity, and since he died only a couple of years after Constantine, there was little opportunity for a period of calm reassessment. We may need to come to terms with the idea that a twenty-first century concept of historical accuracy may not fit very well with a fourth century belief in a spiritual reality.

(As an additional note: - A gold nine-solidus coin was issued in 313 to commemorate the victory of Constantine at the battle of Milvian Bridge. It shows Constantine standing shoulder to shoulder with Sol Invictus: in front of them, a shield showing the galloping sun quadriga — Coin News, February 2018.)

The sign of the cross had an existence long before Christianity, an idea that goes back to Plato, and the gates to pagan heaven could be found where the planetary courses cross the Milky Way. (Perhaps this is what was seen in the sky above Milvian Bridge?) Constantine was converted to Christianity on his deathbed in 337. Now there are two ways of looking at this. In a life that held many sins, it would always make sense to leave conversion, with its wiping clean of the slate, as late as possible. On the other hand, a less sympathetic view has an anxious bishop dashing in to do an emergency conversion job after the Emperor had passed the point of offering resistance. To the end, Constantine had insisted on retaining his title of Pontifex Maximus (High Priest in the pagan world) and coins issued after his death were inscribed DN CONSTANTINUS PT AUGG meaning 'The Deified Constantine, father of the Augusti'. Add the (alleged) story that the prisoners taken at Milvian Bridge were fed to the lions, and that he boiled his wife to death after she falsely accused her stepson of treason, and we have a Constantine who looks firmly pagan.

It became important for Christian thinking to have a clear start-point in the world of Power-Politics and Constantine was clearly the man. Perhaps his religious beliefs needed a bit of post-mortem tidying up, backdated to Milvian Bridge, but Eusebius was keen to promote the view that Constantine was God's primary representative on earth.

ESSAY - CONSTANTINE

It was not long after the Edict of Milan had given Christians the freedom to worship as they wished, that Christians started fighting among themselves, condemning as heretics any Christian group that supported a theological detail slightly different from their own. Add to this a certain amount of unseemly squabbling that arose when it became clear that the office of bishop was an entry to a world of privilege and income.

Looking at Christianity in the early years of the fourth century, we see a world very different from the warm pictures painted at Sunday School. Christians were stretching their new-found freedom and, being Greek, indulging in philosophical debate and wide-ranging argument. It is also worth noting that Constantinople and Alexandria were competing to become leader of the Christian world, with Antioch thinking they had a claim as well. With this as background, we meet Arius, a priest of Alexandria, who was teaching that God created Jesus at a particular point in time (presumably meaning the Annunciation). In my view this looks like a straightforward reading of the Bible, but the Theological Leaders of the day disagreed and condemned poor Arius as a heretic. A goal against Alexandria! But much more than that, it was a turning point in Christianity.

It is difficult to unravel an argument that is nearly seventeen hundred years old, but this is how it looks to me. If you follow Arius, then, from the Beginning of Time, up to the Annunciation, there was no Jesus. For the Theological Leaders, who were promoting a religion based on the person of Jesus Christ, this could not be acceptable. So how about a Jesus who existed for all time in parallel with God and for a small part of that time took on a human form. Good, as far as it went, but it introduces the concept of duality: up, down: good, bad: right, wrong. We talk of an 'open and shut' case when there is no space for further discussion, so duality is not what we want. In any case, duality reminded everybody of the old Gnostic beliefs and nobody wanted that. Try three. God, Jesus and — And what? Try a Ghost. The Holy Ghost. The function of this Holy Ghost, or Holy Spirit, is not easy to understand. Indeed,

I can almost hear the reader thumping the desk — how dare he use the word 'function'! Nevertheless, I see the Holy Spirit as a background, as an atmosphere in which spiritual things can happen. But, most importantly, it avoids the dead-end trap of duality. From now on, we have a Trinity.

In parallel with this theological debate, there was concern of a more political flavour where the hand of Constantine is clear. With the Christian world increasing in size, it became politically desirable that Christians should condense into one coherent body rather than stay as a variety of conflicting arguments. Then the One Government under Constantine could come to an accommodation with the One Church under Jesus Christ and everybody would live happily ever after.

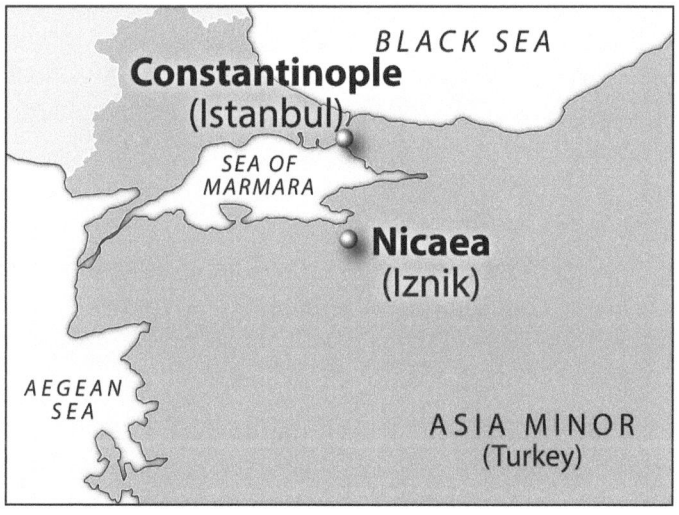

A guide for those unsure about the location of Nicaea.

In 325 Constantine called all bishops to a Council in his palace at Nicaea. It seems that most of the Greeks came, but very few from elsewhere. The object of the council was to achieve unity in the Christian World and to some extent they were successful. They agreed upon a text known from that day to the present as the Nicene Creed. I say, 'to some extent' because a learned clerical gentleman once said to me that this text was the one the majority disagreed with least! The centre of the debate turned on this new idea of Trinity — three parts that combine to make unity — Father, Son and Holy Ghost. It is not difficult to see the problem they faced. Solution of a sort was found in the Greek word HOMOOUSIOS meaning something like "of the same substance". From time to time people have pointed out that this thinking has no basis in the Bible, indeed, the words of Jesus when talking of his Father don't seem to fit the theory at all. However, all this was tidily swept under the carpet and homoousios rules — OK. (Footnote: as well as the word homoousios, the debate included the word homoiousios meaning "of very similar substance". This not only gives us a feeling for the subtlety of the Greek debate, it has left us with a phrase still occasionally heard, "It doesn't matter one iota!")

There were, of course, political undertones to the Council of Nicaea, not least, it was one in the eye for the rapidly increasing body of Christians known as Arian Heretics. Of course, there are no statistics available, but by the latter half of the fourth century I have the impression of an enormous area of central, northern and western Europe filled with Arian Christians. How much of this was spiritual conversion and how much doing what your leader told you — is anybody's guess, but it seems reasonable to think that after a generation or two, Christianity would become part of their culture. But, of course, their culture was illiterate and has left us no records. Meanwhile, back among the very literate Greek Christians a great experiment was progressing. They were gluing together the physical power of a State and the spiritual power of a Church.

For a couple of hundred years Christians had been poor and under attack, but with the coming of Constantine, they gained some sort of freedom and access to money. From the historian's point of view, a poor man leaves little trace, but the rich man leaves records and buildings. Constantine started the tradition of grand churches, with his first being The Church of the Holy Apostles of Jesus in Constantinople, dedicated about 330 and in which Constantine himself was to be buried. Rather more famously, he initiated the building of the great church of St Peter, over Peter's grave just outside Rome, completed about 360.

Constantine's mother, Helena, also initiated the building of churches. Despite being over seventy years of age, around 324, she set out to tour the Holy Land, either to visit the Holy Places, or to seek out the Holy Places (I see the difference as important). Can you imagine a woman, known to have access to all the money in the world, saying to a town clerk in Jerusalem, "Can you show me where such and such an event happened?" The answer has to be "Yes!" She initiated the building of the Church of the Nativity over a grotto in Bethlehem and had a temple to Venus demolished and replaced by the Church of the Holy Sepulchre near Jerusalem. During site clearance, Helena discovered 'The One True Cross' — she actually found three crosses, but she soon identified the True One. Helena returned home in 327, "bringing with her large parts of the True Cross". This record seems to imply someone out there in the misty darkness with a saw. Perhaps the ancestor of those who divided saints up into conveniently sized bits. Again, I have to apologise for confusing modern ideas of historical reality with old stories that may not be true, but do have a real purpose.

So, now we are looking at a Christianity with notable buildings and a power structure. Inevitably, bishops with ambition drifted toward these centres and saw less of the peasants back in the villages. It is worth reminding ourselves that for more than two hundred years Christian worship had taken place in a room within a private house, or standing in the open, around the tomb of someone who had died in Christ, or huddled in a catacomb. In the space of a very few years, the practice of Christianity had changed dramatically.

With organisation improving among and between Christian communities, attention was directed towards the formalised teaching of doctrine. The Doctrine of the Trinity has already been mentioned and we see it becoming something of a spiritual exercise — a sort of religious wrestling match where the concluding result was of less importance that the effort put into the struggle.

Understanding was brought about by the wrestling. I am sure many people, both then and now, come out of their wrestling match feeling better. Certainly Augustine, writing onward from AD 400, found the Trinity to be an 'unimaginable mystery' and his 'De Trinitate' filled fifteen books. But there has to be a problem. Anyone having difficulty with the concept of Trinity (and my earlier remarks suggest where these difficulties might lie) would find that they could no longer call themselves a Christian. Was Christianity intended to draw people together? Well, perhaps. As an aside, the wrestling match mentioned above has similarities with the Zen Buddhist exercise of trying to understand the un-understandable — like the sound of one hand clapping.

Another doctrine that has had enormous effect upon Christianity is the Doctrine of Original Sin. The story goes that God created a perfect world in the Garden of Eden: that a serpent led Eve astray and sin came into the world; since all mankind descent from Eve, sin was built into the system. I have never seen the idea in print, but I get a strong feeling that sex is at the root of the problem. The Church has never really come to terms with the embarrassing and messy process by which human beings produce more human beings. Even more, the Church is a bit afraid of any strong emotions that lie outside Church Authority. Had the Church been in control at the design stage, things might have been very different (Think of the Annunciation and the Immaculate Conception). And so we come to Original Sin. Every new-born child inherits sin through a chain reaching back to Adam and Eve and coloured by the physical processes that brought it to birth. It is therefore desperately important for the soul of this child, to purge this inherited sin by baptism. The Church is in control. Only the Church can free the child from the burden of sin it is said to carry.

Expanding the idea, the Church and its appointed ministers became the only source of teaching and spiritual guidance, to the point where a man can do nothing to aid his own salvation: he is totally dependent upon the Church and the Grace of God. Not surprisingly, at this point, depression sets in and man is surrounded by a black wall of sin and is unable to help himself. This depression shows clearly in Augustine's autobiographical 'Confessions'. In some minds, things get even worse with the concept of Predestination, where the whole world runs in accordance with God's direction and men are but pawns in God's game. Enter the teenage dropout, "Nothing to do with me, Guv!"

This exercise in control by the Church did not go completely unchallenged. Deserving of much more attention than he usually receives, the British monk Pelagius insisted that God had provided man with sufficient wit and intelligence to fight his own battles against sin and look to his own salvation. The attitude of the Church Leaders to this attempt to undermine their authority is best summed up in a comment made by Jerome, the man who wrote the Vulgate version of the Bible. He referred to Pelagius as 'a corpulent dog weighed down with Scottish porridge!' (If you can't win the argument, try insult!)

The great space inside Saint Peter's Basilica, Rome.

The period from the Council of Nicaea (325) to the Council of Constantinople (381) is a period best left forgotten by Christians.

The freedom to worship, confirmed in 313, was soon tossed out of the window and devastating clashes between bishops over politics, personalities and rival theologies were dominant. It is said that more than a hundred people were killed in the competition between Ursinus and Damasus for the office of Pope in 366. (It was Damasus who later commissioned Jerome to write a better Latin translation of the Bible — work that finally became The Vulgate. It was also Damasus who was reputed to have a particular interest in rich women — the smear campaign has a long history!) A whole list of assorted 'heresies' came under fire, but the really intractable problems centred on the relationship between Jesus and His Father. Jesus, as the centre of Christian religion, had to be divine, but in that case He could feel no pain. Mankind's salvation depended upon Jesus suffering on the Cross, so to satisfy human logic, Jesus has to be part divine, part human: so how did He relate to the Father? Nicaea had determined "of the same substance", a Council summoned by Constantius II (Constantine's son) in 359 substituted "like", which set off another bout of hair-splitting. Roman Christians in the West preferred to stay with Nicaea, while the more argumentative East seemed to prefer "like". There is, however, one bright spark in this dark firmament. In 360 Julian took over as Emperor and is well known to students as "The Apostate". From the standpoint of an intelligent pagan he was horrified at the fighting among Christian groups. Unfortunately, he did not live long enough to sort things out.

It is worth a pause at this point, to review what is happening. Both Greeks and Romans had behind them a long history of pagan worship in which, provided a few basic rules were observed (like sacrificing to a recently deceased Emperor), there was quite a lot of tolerance over which god or gods you chose to pray to, and if your neighbour made a different choice, this was not a problem. The coming of Christianity was seen as a departure from a rather casual world into something much more precise, and many priests and bishops seized upon this very search for precision as a tool with which to carve out a distinctive position for themselves and their followers. Inevitably this conflicted with central authority which had always had a preference for uniformity.

The Emperor Theodosius
(379 – 395)

We now come to the Council of Constantinople called by the Emperor Theodosius in 381. Theodosius, born and brought up in Spain, was a soldier through and through, and in facing up to the Goths, had saved the Empire. Compared with Nicaea, this Council was very poorly recorded and seems to have had serious squabbles from start to finish. Although it was called in order for the bishops to resolve matters of theology, it soon became obvious that the official outcome of the Council would be whatever Theodosius wanted it to be. What he wanted was firm adherence to Nicaea (of the same substance). His upbringing in Spain probably gave him a bias in favour of Nicaea. It is worth emphasising at this point that Theodosius spoke Latin and had no Greek and it seems to have been generally understood at the time that Latin was a comparatively crude language which simply did not have the tools to deal with the complex theology that occupied the Greeks. So here we have a man, who didn't understand the question, making a decision that would have a significant effect on most of the people in the western world for more than a thousand years. And most of us have never heard of him!

But it was not the insistence upon the Doctrine of the Trinity as set out at Nicaea that was the world-shaping decision — it was the banning of everything else! We lost the idea of free public debate. We lost the very idea of free-ranging enquiry. You trod the line of approved theology — or else! Even more importantly, a thousand years of Greek study, in a multitude of fields, was tossed into the waste bin, along with 95% of the world's earliest drama, with its comedy and its political criticism. Dark ages — here we come! Fortunately, a small part of this Greek treasure found its way into Arab hands where it was carefully preserved, and at the re-conquest of Spain completed in the fifteenth century, was translated back from the Arabic and slowly became known to the Christian world.

This disciplinarian theology went on to give us some of the darker parts of the Dark Ages with scenes from the torture chambers of hell being painted onto church walls and Christians being given authority to burn other Christians to death if their beliefs were thought to stray from the officially approved set. All for the good of their souls — said through gritted teeth! Church and State had become one body.

As we move into the fifth century we begin to hear talk about the 'Fall of Rome' and it is true that in the year 410, the twenty-six-year-old Roman Emperor Honorius (son of Theodosius) wrote to the Britons telling them to look to their own defence. This is the date usually given for the end of Roman rule, so far as Britain is concerned. But if we stand back a bit and look at the wider picture, we see that Christians in the Roman world had organised themselves into five patriarchates: Constantinople, Alexandria, Antioch, Jerusalem and Rome. We then see that 80% of them were doing all right. It was the Latin-speaking Western Empire centred on Rome that was under attack by barbarous hordes. These barbarous hordes were not the unkempt maniacs beloved by film makers, but moderately well behaved and well organised Christians — but of the Arian sort. (You may remember, going back a number a pages, that the Arians were the ones who preferred a straightforward reading of the Bible, whereas the Authorities in Rome were wedded to Nicene thinking). In fact, the invasions of assorted Goths and Vandals, after the initial shock, did not make a great deal of difference. They took over the reins of power and ran things in much the same way as the Romans had. But remember the Theodosian Rule — Nicaea, good — anything else, bad. A nice touch of symmetry is to be seen when, in 484, Huneric, King of the Vandals, issued a decree against the 'Homousian' heresy of the Romans in his territory.

There are many stories about early Christians that are rarely heard. Either they don't quite fit the organised progression plan wanted by school history books, or they are of little interest to churches, who see church history as the path of their own evolution (or rather, a tidied up version of their own evolution). So I will wind up this section that started with Constantine with a brief look at Nestorius and his Church, roughly a hundred years later.

Nestorius was made Bishop of Constantinople in 428, and like most bishops of his day, he campaigned for the destruction of heresy. One point he made was that to call the Virgin Mary 'Mother of God' was to make her into a goddess and that could not be. He also entered the battle over the degree of humanity within Jesus, and following pressure from Alexandria and from Rome, Nestorius himself was declared a heretic. To me it seems a little sad that here were intelligent men leading a religion that includes the line "love thy neighbour as thyself", doing down anyone they saw as standing in their way to personal advancement, with bullying and bribery as some of the tools in use. Perhaps anyone who proposes the introduction of Christian ethics into the business world of today should take note. It may of course be that bad stories survive better than the good ones, but so be it. Nevertheless, the books of the "lawless and blasphemous Nestorius" were to be sought out and publicly burnt.

There is a point arising from this and other similar disputes. There is something of a problem with the use of the Bible in theological arguments, both then and now; because of its size and variety, careful selection from either the Old or New Testaments can produce a quote for almost any purpose. Fifth century debate therefore tended to bypass the Bible and take their quotes from the Church Fathers — carefully selected Church Fathers. Dare we say it? The word of the Church is becoming more important than the words in the Bible. (Remember Nicaea.) Any document that departed in any way from orthodox was to be burnt and any person found reading such a document was liable for the extreme penalty (Theodosius II, 448). The Church had taken over literature and with it, education, study and thought.

The ideas of Nestorius were formally condemned in 431 and he was deposed and exiled in Antioch in 435. Nestorius and his followers had had enough — they withdrew from the Church and set up one of their own. This is probably not quite true for there was clearly a Christian presence already existing in this eastern region. A Christian bishop is recorded at Merv, out beyond the Caspian Sea in 424 (Merv is near the present town of Mary in Turkmenistan). A date of 431 is given for a split between the Syriac-speaking Eastern Church and the Greek-speaking Church in Constantinople. We are not sure whether Nestorius joined a pre-existing Church or whether he founded a new one, but in either case, it is sometimes referred to as the Nestorian Church, although this is slightly frowned upon today; the preferred name being the 'Church of the East' (sometimes abbreviated, rather confusingly, as 'The C of E'.)

This Church always conducted its liturgy in the Syriac language and it seems to have left behind the raging intolerance that was such a characteristic of the Christian Churches in Constantinople, Alexandria and Rome. It thus seemed able to live alongside other faiths, and this may well be a reason for the phenomenal advance of Christianity across Iraq and Iran, to the nomads of Central Asia, a dip down into Tibet and on into China until stopped by the South China Sea. Bishoprics were established in cities we now know as Beijing and Xian. The nomads got a special dispensation to use mare's milk in place of wine for the Eucharist but what were they to eat in Lent when their only food was on the hoof? A curious situation arose among the nomads of the Central and Eastern Steppes where Christianity was taken up with enthusiasm by the women, whilst the men stayed with their old shamanistic beliefs. As grape alcohol became available, many of the men succumbed to alcoholism and their Christian wives and daughters took over the government of their people.

The territory of the C of E was vast, but it clearly did not have the same density of Christians per acre as in the West. Then in the seventh and eighth centuries Arab Islamic expansion made things more complicated. Nevertheless, all of these areas (with the possible exception of Tibet) still, today, have a significant Christian presence. If we go back to the year 451 and the Council of Chalcedon and pass over the arguments about the natures of Jesus Christ that were still raging, we note that Pope Leo was keen to get it established that his position as Bishop of Rome took precedence over the 'political' capital Constantinople (where all the theological debate had taken place!). The Church of Alexandria decided to split away and form an independent Coptic Church covering Egypt and Eastern Africa.

Thus, in not much more than a hundred years after Constantine's attempt to bring unity to Christendom, the church was in four separate pieces and it would not be much of an exaggeration to say that they would never speak to each other again. The Church of the East and the Coptic Church went their own ways and out of sight, while Rome and the Greek-speaking Church of Constantinople had never had much in common anyway. On a good day in Rome the Greeks were thought to be schismatic: on a bad day they were heretics. Perhaps, and this is speculation, when the western part of the Roman Empire finally drifted to a collapse in 476, the many government offices left empty in Rome were taken up by the

Roman Catholic Church and used to start a new Empire, but this time one based on religion. The cry of "All roads lead to Rome" starts to look like a hopeful publicity shot.

POST SCRIPT

There is a document known as the 'Donation of Constantine' which purports to record the Emperor Constantine handing over to Pope Sylvester (and his successors) political and spiritual authority over Rome and the Western Empire, together with Alexandria, Antioch, Jerusalem and Constantinople. The document itself indicates dates of 315 and 317 but careful study has suggested that it was written in the eighth century. In plain English, it was a forgery. A priest, Lorenzo Valla, published 183 pages of strongly worded criticism in about 1440 that led him and most other people to the forgery conclusion. In the mid sixteenth century, his treatise was placed on the Pope's list of banned books.

AUGUSTINE

The first thing to note is that there are two men called Augustine who make an appearance in early Church history. The first was a theologian who wrote extensively about the Trinity and was made Bishop of Hippo, on the Mediterranean coast of North Africa in 395. This chapter is about the other one.

In the year 597, Pope Gregory, sometimes called 'The Great', sent the monk Augustine to Britain with a mission to convert. (In actual fact, he was sent in 596, but it was the following year by the time he arrived.) So far, so good, and I have no doubt that Pope Gregory did indeed issue this instruction. Unfortunately, many people came to see 597 as an easy answer to the question, 'When did Christianity come to Britain?' So let us have a look and see if we can come up with a more satisfying answer.

We start with a legend. Joseph of Arimathea who was, or might have been, an undercover disciple of Jesus and/or might have been a relative of Joseph or Mary. Might also have been a trader with an interest in tin (at the time, the prime source of tin was in Cornwall). The suggestion goes that on one of his trips to Cornwall, he brought with him the young Jesus. Not a very strong story, but it does give us a great song:

> And did those feet in ancient time
>
> Walk upon England's mountains green?
>
> And was the Holy Lamb of God
>
> On England's pleasant pastures seen?
>
> (Words — William Blake. Music — Hubert Parry)

Moving slightly up the scale of possibility, we meet a story from the pen of The Venerable Bede writing in 731. Bede was a great enthusiast for the Roman Catholic Church and lived at a time when the cross-checking of historical data was far more difficult than it is today, so we need to be a bit careful. Bede records that "In the time when Eleutherius was Pope (around 174 – 189), Lucius, A British King, sent him a letter asking to be made a Christian. This pious request was quickly granted and the Britons held the Faith which they received in all its purity and fullness until the time of the Emperor Diocletian (284)." The thought of a king in Roman Britain rings immediate alarm bells and suggestions have been put forward to place Lucius with native tribes outside the Roman reach — try the Silures in Wales. A book has been published, 'King Lucius of Britain', by David J Knight (2008), which tells a tale of quite surprising complexity, but if I were asked directly, "Was there a Christian Kingdom in Britain in the second and third centuries?" I would have to respond, "Only in fiction!" There might well have been Christian individuals or even groups, but not a kingdom. (As a thought, there might have been a middle-ranking Roman soldier called Lucius Something, who had ideas above his station.)

Still in the third century, we meet St Alban, our first Christian martyr. There seems to be no doubt about his reality, but the date of his martyrdom is very unclear. 208 or shortly after 250 are the present best guesses. There are also stories about the martyrdom of British bishops at the time of the Diocletian persecutions around AD 300. But the first date to give us a real feeling of confidence is 314 when three British bishops were recorded as attending the Council of Arles in southern Gaul. Bishops from York, London and Caerleon. (This, incidentally, was the first Council to be called by the new Emperor, Constantine.)

Archaeology gives us some evidence for Christianity in Roman Britain but not as clearly as we would wish. The mosaic floor found at Hinton St Mary included two roundels, one of Bellerophon riding Pegasus on his way to heaven, and one a portrait bust backed by the Chi-Rho symbol — clearly Jesus Christ — with a pomegranate either side to link with the Roman myths of a descent into the underworld and return. Those who know about Roman hair styles suggest a date around AD 350. So perhaps this is the earliest representation of Jesus Christ anywhere in the world and was found on the floor of a villa in Dorset. The 'house-church' cut into the villa at Lullingstone had painted plaster which, if you believe the patient workers who fitted the broken fragments back together again, including the Chi-Rho and Alpha-Omega symbols. So far as our present study is concerned, the position is fairly clear. After the Edict of Milan (313) took away the threat of persecution, Christians, who were probably quite a small minority, got on with their life and were free to travel and decorate their houses as they wished. Britain was, after all, a long way away from the theologically excitable Greeks.

The Head of Christ
Part of a mosaic floor found at Hinton St Mary in Dorset
Circa 350 AD

One other element may have had an influence on the records. Britain was known by the Roman world to be 'over ocean', in other words, you had to cross the sea to get there: and not just their own personal sea, the 'mare nostrum' or Mediterranean, but the cold, dark, northern sea. From Rome, Britain was seen as the farthest, remotest, coldest part of the known world. Therefore, enthusiasts for the spread of Christianity were keen to talk about Britain. Origen (185 – 254), an early theologian and teacher in Alexandria wrote "When did the land of Britain ever unite in the belief of one God, before Christ came?'

As we move through the fifth century, three processes seem to be unfolding simultaneously. Most obviously, the collapse of the Western Roman Empire following on from military breakdown. Trust, trade and production stopped. Taxes were not collected and without taxes there was no governmental control of the army and before long — no government — no money. If you had cabbages and wanted a sheep, you had to go out and find someone who had a sheep and wanted cabbages. Urban life faded away in Britain, and building with durable materials stopped. The official end to the Empire in 476 when the last Emperor was deposed, went by with hardly anybody noticing.

The second process to unfold in the fifth century had its start at the Ecumenical Council of Constantinople in 381, usually noted as the point at which Christianity became the official religion of the Roman Empire. Actually it was far more dramatic than that: it determined what Christians were to believe and the Church took on powers that started to look very like a police force. And although I can find very little information about how the move happened, the dominant element in Christianity moved from Constantinople to Rome. It may be, as I have suggested elsewhere, that the collapse of the Western Empire left vacant office space in Rome and the church moved in, joining up with the Pope who had been there for nearly four hundred years. Certainly they would be glad to have left behind the arguments and the disputes in Greek. From now on we speak Latin! As Greek was a language for discussion, Latin was a language for command. The Church takes on the word 'Catholic' and assumes authority over all people: and not only people, but any government they might have; and their literature; and their education; and their history. Thus the Roman Catholic Church becomes the principle driving force in Europe for the next thousand years.

The first two of these three processes, the collapse of the Western Empire and the growth of the Roman Church, might be thought of as 'loud', but the third one is very definitely 'quiet'. We begin with the Desert Fathers (it is helpful to relate the word 'desert' to the word 'deserted', rather than just a lot of sand). Somewhere around the year 285 Antony moved out and alone into the Egyptian desert, the better to serve God. Perhaps contrary to his wishes, others came to join him until a hundred years later there were, Mick Aston suggests, five thousand hermits living in the deserts of Lower Egypt. Meanwhile, in Upper Egypt (Upper and Lower relate to the flow of the Nile — Upper, south and Lower, north) these seekers after the religious life came together as communities living under a strict rule of work, prayer and obedience. By 346, Mick tells us, there were nine monasteries and two nunneries in Upper Egypt. The men were called Desert Fathers; I'm not sure about the nuns.

This monastic idea then made an appearance in south-west Ireland. The Gallarus Oratory (a stone built structure the size of a fairly generous garden shed) has a name which might mean something like 'The house or shelter for foreigners'. There is much uncertainty about the date: I would like to think of the 'foreigners' arriving from Egypt or Syria somewhere in the middle 400's and building this stone shelter after their wooden one had rotted and blown away. A couple of similar huts can be found on an offshore rocky islet, Skellig Michael. By the latter part of the fifth century, these quite primitive monasteries were beginning to pop up in remote corners of the British Isles, perhaps initiated by monks from Ireland. A word of warning is necessary at this point: we are dealing with an area now frequently called 'The Celtic Fringe' at a time when deeds of the past were passed down by storytellers and romance was the essential colour. The Venerable Bede recorded (in 731) that St Ninian (whose dates appear to be 367 – 432) established a religious settlement at Whithorn in Galloway, Scotland (before 500). Nothing fits very well where dates are concerned but the overall pattern is, I think, clear. The monastic form of Christianity was spreading around the western shores of Ireland and Britain. (Ninian's name is sometimes given as Saint Nynia and sometimes as Saint Trynnian; a name later used for a notorious, but fictional, girl's school.)

The Gallarus Oratory.
A building in south-west Ireland generally accepted to have a religious purpose, but of very uncertain date.

If we start with Pope Celestine (422 – 432) who is something of a key figure so far as this book is concerned, it was he who excommunicated Nestorius (see the Essay on Constantine) and he sent St Germain to Britain to convert the followers of Pelagius (see also under Constantine and note that some at least of the Britons were Christians although perhaps not of the approved sort). And he also sent the first bishop to Ireland (rather confusingly called

Palladius). Irish readers may be pleased to note that Palladius died and was replaced by Patrick.

Again, we come across a bit of a problem. What were the ideas that Palladius and Patrick carried to Ireland? Good common sense says that they got their instructions from Pope Celestine who must have been a solid follower of Theodosius and the Council of Constantinople, which had by now been formalised as the Roman Catholic Church. On the other hand, all the surviving evidence shows us small monastic settlements in wild and isolated places: ideas that came from Egypt and grew into the Coptic Church which parted from Rome in 451. And again there were niggling differences between these remote foundations and Rome over the method for fixing the date of Easter and over (I kid you not) the style of monastic haircut. Why hadn't Patrick and Palladius sorted these things out? (Unless, of course, these monastic settlements were already up and running for long enough to get set in their ways before Palladius arrived with the latest fashion from Rome.) As all the best books say, "Further research is needed".

Stone huts, with some similarity to the Gallarus Oratory, on an offshore rocky islet, Skellig Michael.

ESSAY - AUGUSTINE

<u>A list of a few of the better known monastic sites of early foundation around the shores of the British Isles</u>

> Whithorn and St Ninian 432, or "sometime before 500".
>
> Iona — founded 563 by Columba who had been exiled from Ireland.
>
> St David's — 6th century foundation.
>
> Bardsey Island — founded 516.
>
> Penmon Priory on Anglesey (St Seriol) — early 6th century.
>
> Glasgow — 6th century foundation by St Kentigern, also called St Mungo.
>
> And possibly the most important: Llantwit Major, South Wales — set up as a school around 500 by St Illtud (450 – 535).
>
> Lindisfarne — not founded until 635 but took its energy from the Irish monk Aiden.

It has to be remembered that almost every one of these early monastic settlements was wiped out by the Vikings, often several times, so little remained of pre-Viking ideas or possessions to feed into the post-Viking re-foundation of the monasteries. And this itself raises another question; if these early monasteries were so materially poor, why did the Vikings raid?

I have tried to outline three of the processes that were shaping Britain at the time Augustine arrived in 597.

> The collapse of the Western Roman Empire.
>
> The setting up and development of the Roman Catholic Church.
>
> The establishment of monastic communities.

ESSAY - AUGUSTINE

Which leaves us with the most obvious — the Anglo-Saxons. Raiders from North Germany had been a problem along the east coast of Britain way back into the third century and the Romans had set up a series of forts along the coast in an attempt to dissuade them. Indeed, the very last message from Britain to the Roman Emperor (410) was a plea for military forces to defend against these Anglo-Saxon raiders. With the final departure of Roman Authority, record keeping is forgotten, but we do have one strong legend. Around the year 449 a British king, Vortigern, worried about the raiders, gave permission for one group of Saxons under the command of Hengist and Horsa to come to this country on condition that they fought off all the other Saxons. It didn't work! Another semi-legend has King Arthur winning a great battle at Mount Badon (somewhere around 518). The military situation eventually stabilised with the Anglo-Saxons in control of the eastern third of the country (and this is the first time we can talk about the land of the Angles, or England).

It was probably news of these pagan Anglo-Saxon incursions that caused Pope Gregory to send Augustine on his way. But, in fact, pagans were probably quite a small minority in Britain as a whole. The western two-thirds of the country had been solidly Christian for two or three generations. Admittedly, some would have been of Pelagian bias and some Arian, but the majority probably didn't care much about such detail. Looking at the eastern third — a country now run by pagan invaders. How many pagan invaders? Well, my guess would be less than 25% of the population. The Anglo-Saxons would have taken over all the military positions, and the control and management jobs, but all the hard work, the ploughing, the milking and the weaving would be done, as it always had been done, by the native Britons and they, like their cousins across the border in the west, were likely to be Christians. I have no doubt that the Pope saw things differently: unless people followed the Roman line in every detail and submitted to control from Rome — they were not Christians. In a very quiet voice can I mention the dozens of monastic settlements around our coasts filled with men of the uttermost devotion to God who yet did not have total agreement with Rome. Indeed, it might be said that they were following God and Christianity in their own way and they may well have seen Rome as irrelevant. But a story like that would never survive a history written by Catholics.

One last thing before we welcome Augustine to our shores. What of the country from which he came — what of Rome? Most people's picture of Rome is centred on the second century when success was in the air, but as the sixth century was drawing to a close, things were very, very different. Population had dwindled and disease was lurking; the secure supply of grain from North Africa had stopped; the sense of being rulers of the world had gone, and the relationship with Constantinople was frosty. The only large organisation still in full flow was the Roman Church and the only means of international communication was to send a bishop. An exaggeration, perhaps, but you get the scene.

Come the dawn of 597, what did Augustine find? History at this point becomes a little bit of a damp squib. Augustine was, after all, a monk, not a military commander, so his progress was slow. Aiming at London, he stopped at Canterbury. Although he would have known nothing about it, a second campaign to convert people to Christianity was being planned up in the far north. With roots in Ireland and working through Iona, spreading down to Lindisfarne, a powerful wave was on the move. Although Augustine and his team achieved conversions and built churches around Canterbury, Rochester and London in a fairly leisurely way, I think it would be fair to say that the rest of the country was more affected by Lindisfarne. Bearing in mind that there were still basic differences between Celtic and Roman practices, it should, perhaps, be noted that at this time, the word 'conversion' could have any of three meanings. Conversion from pagan to Roman: conversion from pagan to Celtic: or conversion from Celtic to Roman. However, none of these processes could be called speedy. Mick Aston notes the conversion of the people in the Isle of Wight in 686, three lifetimes after Augustine. Taking into account the earlier paragraphs, which suggested that the majority of people in Britain/England were already Christian before Augustine arrived, I think that the term 'damp squib' is well justified.

The disagreement between Celtic and Roman supporters rumbled on until a Synod, or official Church Council was called at Whitby in 664, at which a decision was made to follow Rome (because St Peter held the keys to heaven). But still there was no rush. Northern Ireland waited until 700 before accepting the decision; Iona until 716 and Wales until 768. (The terminology is interesting: Iona is described as 'submitting to Rome').

Invading Danes brought back paganism to eastern England around 865 but their paganism didn't last long: a pagan band of Irish Viking adventurers took over land around York, but again, didn't last long. Eric Bloodaxe was expelled in 954: the last example of official paganism in Britain. In 927 the various kings of England and the north drew together under Athelstan with an undertaking to suppress idolatry, and for the first time England became one united kingdom.

As I neared the end of this chapter a sudden flash hit me. Augustine may well have been a very nice bloke, but his actions don't seem to justify his position as a corner-stone of British history. Then — bang — he is the only person with a good, clear and verifiable date. All the other actions take place somewhere within a century or two. All is vagueness — apart from one bright star, Augustine and his date of 597. From the last correspondence with a Roman Emperor in 410, to the Synod of Whitby in 664, dates are very thin on the ground. Welcome to 597!

HENRY VIII

Henry VIII is undoubtedly one of the most talked-about figures in English history. From a tall and handsome teenage prince with all the talents, to a fat and bad-tempered monster, it is a powerful story; then add in six wives and you can sell a library of books. It is usually told as an English story, but I think it should be seen in a wider field than that — much wider.

A first step in widening the view shows the whole of Europe drifting into the control of three centres of power, France, Spain and England, with each centre dominated by one man: Francis I in France (1515 – 1547), Charles I of Spain, who became the Emperor Charles V, the Holy Roman Emperor (1516 – 1556), and Henry in England (1509 – 1547). Three men to run Europe — three long reigns — three men doing the work done today by countless thousands in Brussels and Strasbourg. But, of course, the Europe of Henry's day was very different from now: it was only just struggling out of a backward mediaeval world.

This is clearly no place for a detailed history, but a few salient points might bring us closer to the world as Henry saw it. England was fairly secure within the encircling sea, but the land boundaries in Europe were constantly under dispute. One custom that did much to shape Europe was primogeniture: the oldest son of a lord inherited everything — the title, the land and the money. This meant that estates could remain in a single piece and avoid the breakup into ever smaller bits, but it did leave lots of second, third and fourth sons with a bit of a problem. Of course they could not do work — they were sons of a lord, for heaven's sake! So the only options open to them were the Church, or war. Both should yield, with a bit of luck, a decent income. This enthusiasm for war and glory at any cost was particularly strong among the young men of France. Indeed, that most famous of English victories at Agincourt should, more rationally, be thought of as a grand defeat for the French. All the leading young men of France, dressed in their finery, insisted on being in the front rank, where they were cut down in the first assault. With all those with any wit or authority now dead, or on the ground wounded, all that was left for the English to do was little more than a mopping up operation.

Although trekking across Europe to fight in the Holy Land was no longer a practical proposition (for what it was worth, a peace treaty had been signed with the Mamluks of Egypt in 1370), the word 'crusade' was still very much in people's minds. Any military adventure with a good prospect of plunder was called a crusade and the religion of those to be robbed and killed was largely irrelevant. And if the Pope had given approval, you could earn time off your expected stay in Purgatory. From time to time, cries came from Constantinople for help in repulsing Turkish attacks, but nobody was much interested — there was no money in it. By this time the Roman Church had little interest in the world outside itself and spent much time in theological nit-picking. Did the Holy Ghost proceed from, or through, the Father and the Son? Were there fires in Purgatory? The part of the Christian world that happened to speak Greek, which was of course the part from which most of the Christian ideas had come, was of vanishing insignificance. The imminent prospect of it being conquered by Muslim Turks might get a mention, but action? Pardon me if I yawn. In 1453 the City of Constantine became part of the Muslim world.

If you see the Roman Catholic Church as the mystical body of Christ with the Pope as the head, then there is little more to be said: it is a structure that has no space for comment or criticism. (Remember Theodosius!) And yet it does need criticism.

Although in the modern world we can look back over the Papacy of the last hundred years or so and see little to comment upon. (Perhaps reserving some criticism for Pius XII in his failure to alert the world to the persecution of Jews in Germany.) But, on the whole, Popes have done their job and the Catholic World has chugged along satisfactory. But when Henry looked back at the Papacy from his position in the sixteenth century, he would have seen a very different picture. Still in memory would be the Great Schism (ended in 1417) where there were two, and sometimes three competing Popes, most of whom lied through their teeth in order to

ESSAY – HENRY VIII

keep their position and their wealth. Perhaps the worst was Pope Urban VI who tortured and killed Cardinals and is usually judged to be criminally insane — but he was still Pope!

Maintaining a good and steady inflow of money seems to have been the prime concern of the Papacy, Bearing in mind that they owned something like one third of all the productive land in Europe, this was a good start; then there were the sale of benefices, the notorious sale of indulgencies and, if income looked like falling behind the Pope's expenses, let's have a jubilee and take money from all those pilgrims coming to Rome. And would I be wrong in suspecting that the whole concept of Purgatory was introduced as part of a money-making scheme? Where Popes were elected by Cardinals, and Cardinals were appointed by Popes, here was a system that could very easily slide into corruption, with Popes making their nephews into Cardinals to keep the money in the family. Where ordinary men have sons, Popes have nephews. Apart from the clothing, one begins to wonder whether this money-making operation had anything to do with religion. Boniface IX is said to have died in 1404 "tormented by insatiable greed".

It is perhaps worth noting that back in 1398, frustrated by the two-Pope problem, the French Government decided to ignore the claimant Popes and take control of the French Church into their own hands (along with a suitable share of the money). So Henry was not the first to have this idea. Indeed, twenty-one years earlier than this, John of Gaunt had threatened to secularise the English possessions of the Church, following ideas put forward by John Wycliff.

Moving closer to Henry's own time, we meet Pope Alexander VI (1492 – 1503), the nephew of an earlier Pope and a member of the infamous Borgia family. He achieved the Papacy by extensive bribery, and by having twenty Cardinals among his relatives and friends. He was the father of nine illegitimate children. Then there was Julius II (1503 – 1513) nephew of an earlier Pope. He was followed by Leo X (1513 – 1521) son of Lorenzo the Magnificent, and he had been made a Cardinal at 13. During his Papacy there was extensive selling of indulgencies to help fund the reconstruction of St Peter's. He awarded the title 'Defender of the Faith' to Henry in response to Henry's book defending Catholicism against Luther.

Henry must surely have had a low opinion of Popes and the Papacy: I wonder how he squared this with his clear faith in the Roman Catholic Religion? Rather surprisingly Wikipedia suggests that his wife Catherine, an ardent Catholic, "was aware of what she identified as the shortcomings of the Papacy and church officialdom." Yet another disrupting idea must have been churning around in Henry's mind. His own father-in-law, Ferdinand of Spain, was a leading power in the Spanish Inquisition, that high point of Catholic intolerance.

The period from the late fourteenth century and into the fifteenth was a dark period for the Church. Before that time, it appears that people simply did what the Church told them, without question, but the death of one third of Europe's population around 1349 by bubonic plague planted a seed in the minds of the survivors. They were, after all, the ones who did the work — and provided the food — they had a value! This new thinking began to question some of the Church's customs. Why in the Eucharist did priests get bread and wine when the laity got only bread? The monasteries brewed a good beer for the monks but used later washes through the mash to make small beer for travellers. Then I seem to recall that from around this time the Pope found it necessary to issue a Bull reminding monks that their vow of chastity did extend to prostitutes. Our history books often express shock at the 'Highland Clearances' where poor people in Scotland were expelled from the land by a greedy landlord to make way for more profitable sheep. The monks of the fifteenth century were doing much the same thing, but we don't talk about it. Meanwhile, one tenth of your harvest had to be delivered to the Church's store and the Church sold off the minor church appointments to the highest bidder; but the things that really caused rage were the indulgencies.

The way the system was presented was that the afterlife was divided into three departments. Heaven, where you enjoyed an eternity of happiness along with your equally virtuous friends and the Saints, Jesus Himself and God on His throne. Hell was filled with devils whose only task was to torment you with fire, and where you were fairly regularly torn apart (presumably you would be quietly re-assembled ready for the next tearing-apart session). All this for eternity. Now we come to the tricky bit, the third department, Purgatory. The details of Purgatory are not so clearly defined, but they were definitely unpleasant and you would want to cut down your stay there to the shortest period possible before winning your transfer to Heaven. The length of your stay in Purgatory was determined by your score of sins on earth. (I thought that after Confession you were granted absolution and your slate was wiped clean. Perhaps I have got it wrong.) Anyway, people seemed to die expecting a few years in Purgatory. Back in 1095, Pope Urban II introduced the idea of an indulgence whereby anyone going off to fight in the First Crusade would have their sins remitted and thus their stay in Purgatory reduced or eliminated. On death they would go straight to heaven. (Muslim fighters of today are inspired by the same idea.) So far, so good, but Crusades are expensive, so the idea of an indulgence was extended to those for whom crusading was not an option; the old, the infirm and the female. These people were then able to get the advantages of an indulgence for a simple cash payment (of appropriate size). This scheme was such a success that it went, like income tax, from being a temporary stop-gap, to a permanent feature of the economy. Salesmen ranged across the Christian world selling indulgencies.

This general air of discontent grew, with the churches and monasteries getting bigger and filling up with treasures while churchmen were becoming richer and more distant from the workers who generated the wealth. Some have suggested that an economic tension arose when the gold coinage, intended to facilitate trade, was taken out of circulation and melted down to decorate churches. John Wycliff wrote in 1378, "As the Church was in sin, it ought to give up its possessions and return to evangelical poverty." John Wycliff (1328 – 1384) was a leading academic at

ESSAY – HENRY VIII

Oxford University and as you can imagine, his views did not go down well. However, Oxford was a long way from the centres of religious power, so he did not get burnt (the usual punishment for anyone in serious disagreement with the Church). In Prague University the Czech academic Jan Hus (1370 – 1415) shared many of Wycliff's views, but was not so lucky: he was convicted of heresy at the Council of Constance and burnt at the stake. To make sure, his bones were broken up into small pieces and thrown in the river.

There was another long-standing bone of contention: the Western Church operated in a secret language. A language that was understood by very few common people outside the Church. Thus, when a priest told you (in English) what the Bible said (in Latin) you had to trust him, and trust was running at a very low ebb. We remember the conflict between Rome and the British monk Pelagius back in the fifth century when Rome insisted that a priest was an essential intermediary between Holy Scripture and sinful man. Here we are a thousand years later with the same point being made. If the Church could stop translations of the Bible into English, priests could retain their traditional control.

Bibles in the vernacular languages were beginning to appear in Europe and John Wycliff's translation into Middle English was finished in 1383 — and banned in 1408. William Tyndale's New Testament in modern English was completed in 1526 and three thousand copies printed — but he was found guilty of heresy and possibly strangled and certainly burnt in 1536 with the following as his last words: - "Lord! Open the King of England's eyes!" It should perhaps be noted that the death of William Tyndale in 1536 came after Henry's break with Rome in 1534 but the news had probably not reached him.

I have attempted to put together a picture of the Roman Catholic world as it would have appeared to Henry VIII at the middle of his reign. There is no original research here: all the information is easily available and yet, assembled in this way, the picture looks surprisingly black. A Church and its leaders primarily devoted to money. The Christian teaching used as a tool to keep control over the people and to keep the money coming in. Anyone strong and intelligent enough to upset the system could be accused of heresy and got rid of.

On quiet reflection I think that what we are seeing here is the natural outcome of a bad decision made more than eleven hundred years ago. Theodosius built intolerance into the system, and this intolerance gave us the Dark Ages. The Roman Church grew up through these Dark Ages and the intolerance taught them that anything that varied in any way from their current teaching must be wrong. (See the Essay on Constantine, and its reference to the Council of Constantinople in AD 381.)

Not for the first time I feel the urge to apologise to present day Roman Catholics, although it may perhaps do them good to have a look at where they came from, without the 'tidying up' that inevitably happens to Church history.

Let us now move a little closer to Henry himself. King Henry VIII may be said to have roots going back to Bosworth Field in 1485 where his father won the crown of England. There is much heated debate over this battle, heightened by the recent discovery of Richard III's bones, but there is one factor which seems to me of overwhelming importance. Before Bosworth, it was a mediaeval world in which fighting for power was a normal way of life among those with the money to do it. After Bosworth, with Henry VII's marriage to Elizabeth of York (sister to the Princes in the Tower), the world was a different place: one feels that the world had grown older. There were a number of reasons behind the change: Henry VII saw kingship as a serious management job and kept a close eye on the money. Indeed; towards the end of his life, he became obsessed with money. His wedding, although undertaken with the political aim of blending the houses of Lancaster and York, seems to have been a thoroughly happy marriage (a rare thing among royals). There were, no doubt, those who wanted to return to the rough and tumble of a world before Bosworth but, this being the time of the Tudors, a number of unfortunate accidents were arranged and there was always space in the Tower. Elizabeth got some sort of reward: her picture is still to be found in many homes across the world (she is the Queen in a pack of cards). The world looks forward to an age of discovery, invention and progress!

Here, then, is the Black Ogre that lived in the mind of Henry VIII for most of his adult life. This promising but rather shaky structure of a bright new world post Bosworth could so easily collapse into pre Bosworth mayhem. And it all depended on Henry having a legitimate and healthy male heir and, bearing in mind the health risks of the day, a second back-up or Duke of York. (Henry had himself been the back-up to his elder brother Arthur.)

Queen Catherine of Aragon

ESSAY – HENRY VIII

The story of Arthur's death and Henry's getting a special Papal dispensation to marry his brother's widow is well known (Arthur died aged 15). Whilst waiting for Henry to grow up a bit, Catherine of Aragon was appointed Ambassador for the Spanish Court, the first female ambassador in European history, so she was intelligent as well as being unusually good looking. Henry was nearly eighteen when he became king in 1509 and married Catherine a few days before his coronation. She was twenty-three (we are talking fertility, so female ages are important). Catherine went through six pregnancies, 1510, 11, 13, 14, 16 and 18. So Henry and indeed Catherine were clearly doing their best. It was their misfortune that only one child lived more than a couple of months: the 1516 birth of Mary. After living together for sixteen years and the Queen approaching forty, Henry felt it necessary to look elsewhere for his dream of a legitimate male heir. That word 'legitimate' meant that he had to divorce Catherine and marry a younger wife. His eye fell upon Anne Boleyn (he had already had a son by her sister Mary in 1526, probably) but first things first — the divorce. Divorce is seldom easy, but this one was difficult beyond all reason. His wife was passionately opposed, and since the wedding had been by special dispensation of the Pope, he had to go back to the Pope to ask for a divorce. The Pope at that time was a prisoner of the Holy Roman Emperor Charles V, following the sack of Rome in 1527, and Charles just happened to be a nephew of Queen Catherine.

It is useful at this point to give a thought to the Pope who was in receipt of Henry's request. Pope Clement VII, 'The Second' (yes, there were two Popes Clement VII) was the illegitimate son of Giuliano de Medici and nephew to Lorenzo the Magnificent. He had been made Cardinal by his cousin Pope Leo X (Lorenzo the Magnificent's son). You must already be getting the impression that this was a family affair amongst Florentine bankers, who were unlikely to be much impressed by Henry's problem. Enter Emperor Charles V. Arguments about overlordship of Central European territories were frequent, and at this particular time, Charles was leading a large army into Northern Italy to prove some point or other. Unfortunately, the money ran out. When an army is not being paid, it tends to look for other sources of income. In this case, it saw Rome. For six weeks and more, Rome underwent a full-scale mediaeval sacking. All portable wealth was taken away and some reports claim that three quarters of the buildings were destroyed and many thousands killed. Many people held the Pope responsible for his failure to organise a defence plan. Indeed, when he died in 1534, one story tells of a plan to have his body dragged through the streets of Rome impaled on a meat-hook.

I have just said that Pope Clement was a prisoner of Charles V, but that requires a little refinement: Clement was a prisoner of Charles V's army, but the army had mutinied and was no longer under Charles' control. Thus, for around six months, the army held Clement, and Charles had to make apologies to the other heads of Europe. When the mutineers had advanced upon Rome, Clement made use of a protected corridor that led from the Pope's apartments in the Vatican to the much more secure Castel Sant' Angelo. (One does wonder who thought it appropriate to construct such an escape route?) In due course, the Pope was captured, and he offered 400,000 ducats for his life. By the end of 1527 Rome's population was down to 10,000, the food had run out and plague had arrived. So why had the Pope not given more attention to Henry's divorce? You don't need to ask!

Without any co-operation from Rome, Henry declared his own divorce and married Anne, with this marriage confirmed valid in May 1533. Also in 1533, Henry was excommunicated for the first time. Anne bore Elizabeth after eight months of marriage and went on to have certainly one miscarriage and maybe more. The story that she miscarried a son on the day of Catherine's funeral may or may not be true.

The best known name in the Protestant Reformation is of course Martin Luther, a German monk and Catholic priest who was a close contemporary of Henry VIII. Luther was eight years older and died in 1546, Henry died in 1547. At the centre of Luther's campaign was opposition to the sale of indulgences and his belief that the

Bible was the only source of divinely revealed knowledge and should be available for ordinary people to read.

The situation in England was very different. The matter of Henry's divorce makes a good story and perhaps takes too dominant a place in many history books: I would rather see it as a sad tale that just happened to coincide with greater matters. Matters of Authority and Money. Matters that had been around for a long time, but were just beginning to come to the boil.

Going back into the fourteenth century, Popes and the Papacy had been doing their best to establish the superior authority of the Church above Kings and Governments. They did not succeed, at least as far as political power was concerned, but they did manage to hold on to a large part of the money flow. Thus, when we come to the English Reformation, we see something that looks very like the financial aspects of winding up a large company: very little to do with religion. Flows of money were redirected from Rome to the Crown account. Henry made a charge on the Church in Canterbury of £100,000 to release them from their obedience to Rome (the legal reasoning may be obscure, but the sum of money was real enough — say times 300 to give a modern idea). Finally, in 1534 the 'Act of Supremacy' was passed by Parliament and Henry became head of the Church of England. We need to remind ourselves that although England had a Parliament, in all important matters Parliament did what Henry told them. So it is not far from the truth to say that England, under Henry VIII, was a dictatorship. Certainly, anyone who crossed this path, or simply fell out of favour, could expect a charge of either treason or heresy. Do you prefer to be hung, drawn and quartered, or to be burnt at the stake? Life under the latter part of Henry's reign, when he was grossly overweight and suffering continuous pain from ulcerated legs, was risky for anyone in authority or, indeed, for anyone who spoke in public.

So, what was the difference between living under a Roman Catholic Church, and living under a Church of England ruled by Henry? The immediate response is 'Not a lot'! The religious world was still hard at work bickering as much as always. You could still get yourself burnt for refusing to believe that the bread of Communion turned into the Body of Christ. One word sums up the world of religion both before and after Henry's take-over — Intolerance!

It seems to fit the evidence if we assume that Henry saw separation from Rome as a purely financial matter. We have already noted his re-direction of the money flow and his charges put upon Canterbury, but the big item was the wealth represented by the monasteries and their land. Many scurrilous tales have been told about dodgy goings on in the monasteries and by way of balance, stories of the help, support and education that the monks provided for the local communities. Bearing in mind that there were nigh on a thousand religious houses, there were probably some of all sorts. But to Henry, they all represented money, and he wanted it.

In 1539, half-way through the process of confiscating the monasteries and their land, Henry promoted 'The Statute of Six Articles' which confirmed that, so far as worship and belief were concerned, we were all to follow closely on the Roman pattern. It was as though the English Reformation had never happened. Yet Henry was far from satisfied with the performance of his church and the behaviour of his government. On Christmas Eve 1545 Henry made what was to be his last speech to Parliament: full of strong criticism for their lack of charity.

> "My loving subjects: Study and take pains to amend one thing which surely is amiss and far out of order, to the which I most heartily require you which is that charity and concord is not amongst you but discord and dissentions beareth rule in every place."
>
> "Alas! How can the poor souls live in concord when you preachers sow amongst them in your sermons debate and discord? To you, they look for light and you bring them darkness."

ESSAY – HENRY VIII

"You of the temporality be not clean and unspotted of malice and envy, for you rail on bishops, speak slanderously of priests and rebuke and taunt preachers, both contrary to good order and Christian fraternity."

(Quotations taken from Robert Hutchinson's book "The Last Days of Henry VIII")

This all seems eminently reasonable criticism and then one reads the appalling case of Anne Askew, eight months later. Anne was another who had trouble with the doctrine of transubstantiation. She debated the matter with priests and officials and was finally taken to the Tower where she was broken on the rack and then carried to Smithfield where she was tied to a stake and burnt.

It seems clear that Anne's crime was her intelligence. For anyone to debate with a priest was bad enough — but a woman! Once more we see the lead weight tied round the neck of Christianity by Theodosius. What the Church says is right: all else is, by definition, wrong and should be destroyed.

Let us try to summarise by painting a rough picture of life in England in the later years of King Henry's reign (1530's and 1540's). The great majority of ordinary people were living in close contact with the land, dependant on weather and harvest and luck, without any of our modern ideas about the way the world works. Their only guide was what the Church told them — and I have no doubt that horror stories circulated about the men who had strayed away from the Church's path. Magic and witchcraft lurked in the background. Everyday life was coloured by the Church to a degree few people today would understand.

The World (meaning the Western European world) was what the Roman Church had made it: a world created by God, redeemed by Jesus Christ and administered from Rome: the whole structure held together by faith and, some might add, discipline, strengthened by a Latin language well suited to command. Since there was no question that Rome and its teaching were right, there could be no space for alternative thinking. You were either a good Catholic; or you were wrong! Ships may have been getting bigger, but still the human mind was confined to ideas a thousand years old! There was, of course, comfort to be drawn from living with old ideas: the comfort of an old armchair. Henry himself liked the old armchair. He was outraged by Luther's attempts to stir things up, so he wrote a book defending the Seven Sacraments against Luther's attack. For this, Pope Leo X awarded Henry the title 'Fidei Defensor' (Defender of the Faith) and the letters 'Fid Def', or 'F.D.' have appeared on our coins from 1714 to the present day. It is my firm belief that Henry retained his conviction in the theological rightness of the Roman Church up to the day he died. But he was King: he had a duty to run things in the best interests of his country.

If I believed in the devil, I would see him looking up at Europe in the fifteenth and sixteenth centuries and saying to himself, "This Christian lot have become boring: no excitement! But I have a key to challenge Saint Peter's — money!" It would clearly be going much too far to suggest that the Reformation was the work of the devil, although some Catholics might see it in that way, but we should feel some sympathy for Henry, who was torn between his life-long belief, and his duty as King to separate England from the money whirlpool that had developed in Rome. This was the root of the protest that gave us the word 'Protestant'. It was not Henry, but two of his children who introduced religious fanaticism into our history books.

CHAPTER NINE
SOME REFLECTIONS ON THE EARLY DAYS

The essays on Constantine, Augustine and King Henry VIII bring to an end the original objectives of this book, but I find myself left with a few half-formed ideas that will not lie down. Among these ideas is a curiosity about the earliest days of Christianity.

Jesus died in the year 30 (plus or minus a year or two) but it is not until the Council of Nicaea in 325 that Christianity takes on the sort of written record that makes historians feel comfortable. Two hundred and ninety-five years! The same span of time that separates us from our new German-speaking King, George I. At this point any fully committed Christian will throw his hands in the air and claim that all we need to know about this early period is contained in the New Testament! Well, possibly. The NT tells us that Jesus was born "In the days of Herod the King" (Matthew 2:1). We are also told that the tax which was central to the events surrounding Christ's birth, "was first levied when Cyrenius was Governor of Syria." (Luke 2:2). Now Herod died in the year 4 BC and Cyrenius was not made Governor of Syria until AD 6. So there is a bit of a problem, but if we accept that the Gospels were set down in writing seventy, eighty or even more years after the Nativity, then slightly shaky memories are not a surprise.

Back in Chapter Four, it was mentioned that the writing of the Gospels seems to have happened at a surprisingly late date. Nothing is known for certain, but the table offered by Lena Einhorn in her book, 'The Jesus Mystery' gives a set of dates for the writing of the four Gospels that seems to be in line with recent thinking.

Mark	68 — 73	Approx.
Matthew	70 — 90	Approx.
Luke	80 — 100	Approx.
John	90 — 110	Approx.

It is possible, I suppose, that Mark was five years younger than Jesus and started the writing of his Gospel when he was sixty-three, but this sort of idea becomes increasingly unlikely for the others, particularly if we accept the story that John was the only disciple to live out a full life and die a natural death. Nothing is certain, but we are being pointed towards a situation that has a number of important consequences.

The traditional and comfortable view sees the Gospels written by four men who were in close daily contact with Jesus himself. But if this new look at the dates is correct, then the Gospels were written by the next generation, or even by the children of the next generation: written perhaps by people born long after the Crucifixion, who were setting down the stories told by elderly friends or found on old pieces of writing. These four unknown men (I assume they were men) were later awarded the courtesy titles of 'Matthew', 'Mark', 'Luke' and 'John'. This version of how the writing came about does something to account for the rather scrappy arrangement of the stories within each Gospel (and for the variations between them). It might also explain the absence of any feeling of personal warmth that might have been expected if the writer had been a close companion of Jesus. Yet another consequence would be that Paul becomes the earliest of the Christian writers; pre-dating the Gospels. Again, the later gospel writers would surely have searched among the old texts and it would be a strong man who could resist fitting a gospel story on to an old prophecy. The picture we seem to have these days of Mary, in the latter stages of pregnancy, riding sixty-five miles on the back of a donkey in order to give birth in a place associated with King David, might be a result.

If we pause for a moment and think of the Land of Israel: its geographical position seems to be a generator of unrest: it was 'leaned on' by its neighbour Persia, and then by the Greeks following the expansions of Alexander the Great in 330 BC. A period of comparative quiet then built up into a full-scale revolt in the 160's BC, led by Judas Maccabaeus. The Jews won their independence but the internal squabbling went on and on until somebody had the bright idea of asking the Romans if they could help. The Romans were happy to oblige and moved in in 63 BC. The interest of the Romans had always focused on towns: the countryside had very little to attract them — and Israel was mostly countryside. The Romans therefore delegated authority to a local king and, moving into our period of interest, that King was Herod the Great.

Now King Herod may have been a fairly nasty piece of work in many ways, but he was a Jew, and he held the Jewish people together reasonably well. Then, on his death in 4 BC, the land for which he had been responsible was divided between three of his sons with Galilee coming under the control of Herod Antipas and Judea under Archelaus. Archelaus was not up to the job and after ten years he was sent into exile by the Romans and a Roman administrator put in his place. From the year 26, this administrator (or Prefect, or Procurator) was Pontius Pilate. Once again there was pressure for a move towards Jewish independence and a handful of men came to the fore claiming to be 'The One' to lead the Jewish people to political and religious freedom, and the label 'Messiah' was claimed on more than one occasion. One such group, the Zealots, adopted a militaristic policy, becoming ever more fanatical until a full-scale Jewish revolt against the Romans broke out in the year 66. The Romans recognised the seriousness of the situation and responded with heavy military force which knocked the stuffing out of the Jewish people. A few Zealots survived for a while in the hills, but by the year 70, it would not be much of an exaggeration to say that the picture of an independent Jewish nation lay broken on the floor.

This brief sketch of Jewish history is intended to paint the background behind the life of Christ. We see a fairly stable Jewish community at the time of his birth; followed by a period of some confusion when Herod's sons had taken over; then the firm, but rather reluctant hand of Roman administration in Judea, mixed with the surviving religious leadership in Jerusalem. Then, after the

SOME REFLECTIONS ON THE EARLY DAYS

crucifixion, the age-old quest for Jewish independence becomes active again, leading to revolt and to a crushing defeat by the Romans.

If we now turn our minds back three or four paragraphs —. When was it that the story of Jesus was written down? If we accept the suggestion of dates between 68 and 110, as mentioned above, then, to use an old expression, a lot of water had flowed under the bridge between the teaching and the execution of Jesus, and the writing down of his story. Forty years of dramatic change. (Just think for a moment of the difference between the England of 1910 and the England of 1950.) So the gospel writers were working and living in a very different world from the one they were describing. Jesus had lived in a fairly calm and essentially Jewish society, whereas the gospel writers were in a more obviously 'occupied' world, with a pagan Roman authority breathing down their necks.

The crucifixion of Christ may well be the most carefully studied event in all history. (With a brief apology to those who do not consider it to be history.) It is strange, therefore, that there are so many 'oddities' embedded within the story. A first response might be to put it down to careless translation; but this material has been gone over countless times by people with wide-ranging objectives, so I am quite confident that our King James version fairly represents what was written down in the Gospels. But the early part of this chapter has suggested there may be a substantial gap between the crucifixion, and the writing down of the story, of forty to eighty years. Did the oddities creep in during this gap?

To start with, the primary accusation against Jesus seems to be that he had claimed to be 'The King of the Jews'. Now, thirty years earlier, the Romans had been very happy to work alongside a King of the Jews (Herod); so what had changed? Did they now think that, just possibly, Jesus was one of King Herod's descendants with an undercover intention to take over the Jewish people? (Where would such a thought place Joseph and Mary? Was she perhaps Princess Mary? It might however offer an explanation of how Jesus had escaped the 'slaughter of the innocents' without needing a journey

SOME REFLECTIONS ON THE EARLY DAYS

into Egypt.) Then, on a quite different point, crucifixion was a punishment regularly used by Romans against offending non-Romans: they knew how it worked: the victim hung on the cross for two or three days before dying; this was the horror of the punishment. Why then did the Romans initiate the crucifixion of Jesus on the day before Passover if there was a requirement that bodies must not remain on crosses on the Sabbath Day? (i.e. the next day.) Or, yet again, there seems to have been four candidates for crucifixion at this time; Jesus himself, Barabbas, found guilty of insurrection and murder, and two thieves. Now we are told that there was a custom, in the run up to Passover, for one prisoner to be released back to the people (although there is no confirmation of such a custom from any source outside the Gospels, and a spark of democratic choice under a Roman authority does seem a little bit unlikely). It would appear that theft was a lesser crime than insurrection and murder, and yet the two thieves do not seem to have been considered for the possibility of release. The choice was between Jesus and Barabbas. Now in the Jewish language, 'Bar' means 'son of' and 'Abbas' means 'father', so the question as put to the crowd would have been, 'Do you want The King of the Jews? Or do you want The Son of the Father?' As we all know, they chose The Son of the Father. Were the audience confused? Jesus died on the cross after six hours, just after having been given a drink. Many authors have attempted to provide an explanation for these events that did not depend upon Divine Intervention. Lena Einhorn is perhaps the most adventurous: she sees Jesus being given a drugged drink that gives him the appearance of death: being taken away and concealed while he recovered, then re-appearing some while later on as Saint Paul. I make no comment on this and other similar stories, but they must lead both writers and readers to a closer study of their Bible, and this is probably a good thing.

Before I leave this topic, there is one glaring oddity that must be included here. Joseph of Arimathea took the body of Jesus after the crucifixion then, later, in company with Nicodemus, they "Came to Jesus by night, and brought a mixture of myrrh and aloes, about a hundred-pound weight." (John 19:39). Several points arise. Firstly, it would take an unusually strong man to carry a hundred pounds: even if they had half each, fifty pounds would still be quite a challenge. Secondly, what about cost? One thinks of myrrh as among the rare fragrances and spices: a quick flip through Google suggests a present day price around £5 an ounce — say £4,000 for the myrrh half of a 50:50 mix with aloes. OK, the figures are modern and don't mean very much, but they do suggest that myrrh, both then and now, was a very expensive material. (Why else would a King bring an offering of myrrh to the baby Jesus?) So Joseph and Nicodemus were carrying something that was very heavy and very expensive. What were they going to do with it? My suspicious mind suggests that a hundred-pound weight is quite likely to match the weight of Jesus' body (7 stone, or 45 kilos). Was there a substitution planned? Was the sack marked 'myrrh/aloes' actually containing sand? The thought of how such a large quantity could be utilised for any legitimate/orthodox purpose is so baffling that the mind is left to follow unorthodox trails.

Moving on, there is something to be seen in the events that followed the great fire of Rome in AD 64. Towards the end of his reign, Nero slipped over the edge into insanity and many people thought that the fire had been deliberately started by Nero himself — presumably in order to clear the ground and make space for his latest building ideas. With suggestions like this in the air, Nero looked around for someone to blame. His eye fell upon the Christians. The important point for us to notice here is that Christians were present in sufficient numbers and were sufficiently distinctive to provide Nero with the target he was looking for. So, here in Rome, some years before the gospels were written down (probably), there was a noticeable Christian community. The letters of Paul show us where there were other Christian communities, but it is in Rome that we get a hint of substantial size. So, how was Christianity taught in those days before the gospels? Back in Chapter Five there was some mention of the very early days when God's Kingdom was seen as just around the corner and martyrs were doing no more than taking a short cut. Urgency was in the air. Teaching was spread by quick words in dark corners and by nervous meetings in locked rooms (probably). The calm solidity of a written gospel was some long way off into the future. The excitement of these early days might remind us that Christians and Jews were still quite close, indeed, many Christians would have been born into a Jewish family. And some of the Jewish teaching, handed down from the prophets, carried a similar sense of excitement. I once worked with a colleague who had fought with the Polish underground resistance during the second world war and he told of a life that was both exciting and dangerous. Everybody with a secret name; nothing written down, and an attempt, constantly being made, to wipe out from the mind any memory of faces or places in case you were captured. This might give us something of an insight into the world of a Christian community living in Rome around the year 60. It would certainly explain the absence of any writings from this period, and although both Peter and Paul are thought to have been there, there is no evidence.

Paul had travelled around the eastern Mediterranean as described in the 'Acts of the Apostles' and ended up in Rome, so we can reasonably assume that 'Acts' was written in Rome. If Paul's journeying had been in the 40's and perhaps into the 50's, then it seems likely that the writing up of his story happened in the late 50's, before the Christian community in Rome had become big enough to be a political target. This idea takes on an extra importance if we accept that 'Acts', written by Paul (or perhaps by Luke, or perhaps by the two of them together) is the oldest piece of writing in the New Testament: indeed, the oldest piece of Christian writing FULL STOP! Many years ago it seemed to me that Paul was over represented in the New Testament. We were told of the twelve Apostles in daily contact with Jesus; four of them going on to write the familiar gospels. And there was an expectation that these twelve would spread out across the world, taking Christ's teaching to all who wanted it and creating the Apostolic succession. With such a scenario Paul, a man who never actually met Jesus

SOME REFLECTIONS ON THE EARLY DAYS

(apart from in a vision), should be little more than a figure in the background. But if, as we now suspect, the four gospels were written later by somebody else, and the stories of travel by the Apostles look to be written with more imagination than fact, then Paul, his letters and the 'Acts of the Apostles' take on an earlier, and therefore a more dependable appearance.

Back in Chapter Four there was mention of the travels and adventures of Apostles which, one feels, ought to have been happening in the 40's and 50's, but their stories do not carry the same sort of reality that we find in 'Acts'. I have no evidence, but I get the feeling that these travelling Apostles were teaching a Christianity that was still very close to the Jewish faith. Paul, on the other hand, was teaching Christianity as a completely new religion. Perhaps we should remind ourselves yet again that the object of Christians at this time was to survive, and to spread the Gospel: any attempt to record events or to construct a history must be put off until later. (In James' case, very much later. It seems that his journey to Spain happened in the ninth century!)

The worlds in which Christianity grew up, Israel, then the Greek world, then Rome, were all notably literate societies, at least at the higher social levels. It has raised comment as being rather strange that there is so little (or no) mention of Christ, or of the events surrounding him, in the many accounts or histories written about the first century. There is one notable exception to this idea: in a book, 'Antiquities of the Jews' by Josephus, there is one paragraph that tells of Jesus as a 'doer of wonderful works'; Pilate 'condemned him to the cross', and to those that loved him, 'he appeared to them alive again the third day'. Unfortunately, this paragraph has no connection at all with the preceding, or the following paragraphs. In other words, it is almost certainly a later insertion by an unknown hand. The Bible is telling us of a major event involving the senior Roman Official of the day and the 'top brass' of the Jewish religious community in Jerusalem, all involved in a situation that could so easily be read as the start of another

Jewish revolt. And yet no non-Christian writer thinks it worth a mention!

Just one small footnote: thirteen years after the crucifixion, the Roman army invaded Britain. Perhaps historians found this to be more interesting than yet another Jewish revolt that didn't quite take off.

Perhaps it came by Peter; perhaps it came by Paul, but the arrival of Christianity in Rome was one of the great events of human history. It may have taken two and a half centuries to get established, but it grew to fit like a right hand in a right hand glove. Rome was in a location that gave natural access to both the Mediterranean world and the cooler climates of western and northern Europe where activity was encouraged by the weather. Rome had a long tradition of organised government backed up by a sound legal code and a system of taxes that provided the money so that officials and soldiers all got paid. A good recipe for stability. And Rome had a remarkable language: clear, precise, and not weighted down with complexity: a good language for issuing commands and instructions.

Now Christianity came from the lands of Galilee and Jerusalem; lands where the One God of Judaism had been well established for many centuries. Christians arriving in Rome had to face up to a very different situation. They found a multitude of gods; offerings to the living Emperor, and little regard for the worth of human life. The Romans could be tolerant of other people's religions, provided that occasional offerings to the Emperor were made, and I am sure that Christians who kept their heads down would have been all right, but it is part of a Christian's belief to stand up and be counted, and public meetings and preaching would have attracted unwelcome attention where some of the emperors were constantly on the lookout for victims for the arena. Not surprisingly, the historical record has little to say about Christians in Rome before the abdication of the last anti-Christian Emperor, Diocletian, in 305. Things then happened in a rush. 312 saw the victory of Constantine at the Battle of Milvian Bridge, and the Edict of Milan the following year gave Christians the freedom to worship as they wished; then 314 saw the first international Council for Christian bishops and in 324 Constantine moved his capital from Rome to Byzantium, changing its name to Constantinople, and he started the Christian tradition of building grand churches. But something of Rome seemed to travel with the move, for although the inhabitants of Constantinople spoke Greek, they referred to themselves as 'Romans', and Constantine himself was thoroughly Roman.

However, the Pope did not move: he stayed where he had always been: and later on Pope Leo (440-461) was keen to emphasise that ultimate religious authority rested with him, in Rome! Thus, when Christianity took on something of a formal structure at the First Ecumenical Council (held in Constantine's palace at Nicaea, in what we, today, call Turkey) its shape was directed by Constantine with his strongly Roman background.

As the military might of Rome declined in the fifth century, there seems to have been a drift of Church Authority back from the Greek world of Constantinople, back to Rome. And two words became linked together to influence a large part of human history — 'Roman Catholic'! The word 'Roman' has an obvious meaning, but 'Catholic' is also important. My dictionary offers, "Universal; of interest or use to all men; all-embracing —." An excellent label for a church with aspirations. (I am reminded of a small group of Russian revolutionaries who called themselves 'The Majority'.) When reading accounts of early Christianity (say from the Council of Nicaea and onward for the next thousand years) it is very easy to get the feeling that the Roman Church was indeed universal. There may have been the odd hiccups with heretics, but generally speaking, the Church issued the instructions and the people did what they were told. But then, we are looking back on an organisation that produced its own records and those records show that it was very successful — provided we ignore the Christian Churches of Greece and of Eastern Europe and the Arians of Western Europe; the Churches of North Africa and Ethiopia, of Iraq, Iran and China — then yes: the Roman Catholic Church was indeed all-embracing! But, in spite of these salutary reminders it is plain to see that the Roman Church is still a powerful force in the world around us today.

It is worth remembering that Rome had been a centre for power and authority for hundreds of years and people had grown accustomed to living under Roman rules so, when her military power faded in the fifth century, it is quite easy to see Christianity picking up the bones of the dying giant and inheriting a position of authority. Among those bones was the Latin language, a good practical language that had spread across the empire: those who could write, wrote Latin. So Christians moved away from the complexities of Greek, and took up Latin. The Universal Church now spoke with the Universal Language!

This choice of Latin as the 'Top' language was to set a pattern in the Western world that was to last for fifteen hundred years. As the Roman way of life declined through the fifth and sixth centuries the Latin of everyday use faded away to be replaced by local or tribal languages, thus the Church found itself teaching in a language that was not understood by most of its members. However, this obvious disadvantage was balanced by a great sense of 'mystery' that was a strong component in the mediaeval mind and the Church came to be seen as a powerful and mysterious body with authority over all aspects of life and death. Thus we begin to see a division of society into two parts: the Church and its ministers, bound together with Kings and Princes and those capable of intelligent thought — a group defined by the Latin language. On the other side of the fence were the workers; the ones who spoke the local language; the ones who produced the food that kept everybody going. (The roots of modern politics go back a long way!) In passing, it is interesting to see this fairly natural development into a two-part society, and I have little doubt that comparisons would have been made with the old-fashioned religious beliefs of the early Christian Gnostics (where God lived in an upper spiritual world while ordinary mortals lived in the lower material world of everyday work). It was important to the Roman Church to be seen as different from its

Gnostic predecessors, so out with two part thinking and in with three parts — welcome to the Trinity!

From Nicaea to the present day 'The Trinity' has been an important feature of Christian teaching: (last week I went to church on 'Trinity Sunday'). The first thing that needs to be said is that the Trinity is not a teaching from the Bible: Jesus refers to His Father as a separate individual in much the same way as you or I might refer to our fathers. And yet there are bookshelves, indeed whole libraries full of books about 'The Trinity': Father, Son and Holy Ghost. I have neither the ability nor the wish to review this material, but there are a few thoughts that might usefully be mentioned here. In the everyday world dualist thinking suggests that weight depends on 'size' and 'material': Trinitarian thinking offers 'size', 'material' and 'gravity'; thereby offering a deeper understanding of the mysterious world around us.

It is a long-standing characteristic of Christian teaching that the words are chosen to make sense for all levels of spiritual awareness. A parable might be read as a simple story: it makes some sort of sense even for those who miss the spiritual message. However, other religions have a different approach and do not bother about intelligibility at street level. "Tao begot the One; the One, the Three, and the Three, everything!" And one feels tempted to add, "And he that has ears to hear; let him hear!"

Three-dimensional thinking is a step closer to the real world, whether your interest be physics or theology, it is a move away from pictures and words and out into the fresh air of experience. A dualist lives on a train — he can go one way; or he can go the other. But the Trinitarian has a bicycle — he can go anywhere he likes.

Let us face it, this is an area of thought and spirit that is difficult (impossible) to put into words. The Church following Constantine chose to represent the real but indescribable as a family relationship "Father, Son and Holy Ghost", and the fact that Church people are still puzzling about it seventeen hundred years later suggests that they made a good choice.

UNFORTUNATELY, we next come to the soldier/Emperor Theodosius and his Council of Constantinople in 381. (Refer also to the Essay on Constantine.) Theodosius was faced by a world that was falling apart: his victory over the Goths had brought a temporary halt to the collapse of Roman military authority, but the signs were fairly clear that the 'Roman World' was coming to an end. As he saw it, there was but one ray of light: the rising authority of the Christians. Constantine had done much to establish a clear path for Christianity and separate it from some of the wilder heresies: he had also created an important connection between Church and State. Theodosius now felt the need to go further: religion needed to be tightened up! He dissolved the ages old tradition of the Vestal Virgins and put an end to the pagan festival known as 'The Olympic Games' (last Games, 393). Religious persecution came back onto the scene, only this time it was Christians doing the persecuting: Theodosius dismissed anyone who would not accept the Nicene Trinity as 'Foolish Madmen!' (As a curious aside, he gave orders to transport an old and very pagan obelisk of Thutmoses III — originally from Karnak — from Alexandria to Constantinople. This moving of two or three hundred tons of Egyptian obelisk has happened with surprising frequency throughout history. I assume it was seen as a challenge; a way to demonstrate strength. A splendid example stands centre-stage in front of St Peter's in Rome!)

At his Council of Constantinople (and it was very much 'his' Council) the target was to focus Christianity on the pattern set at the earlier Council at Nicaea fifty-six years earlier. Theodosius was insistent that 'The Nicene Creed' and the 'Doctrine of the Trinity' was the way to go. Then, almost without noticing it, he dropped a bombshell! So important were these Christian ideas that any other interest or study was a waste of time and a distraction. Out with the rival Christian heresies: out with pagan ideas, and because they were pagans, out with the works of Socrates, Aristotle and Plato and out with the works of the Greek playwrights who had shown so much understanding of the ways in which communities and governments functioned. Not only were these works out of favour: they were physically destroyed. A thousand years of human development tossed out of the window and on to the bonfire! Not only did Theodosius affect the thousand years before him, he also affected the thousand years that came after — think of the problems of Galileo and Darwin. Not until the reign of Queen Victoria did the sciences begin to free themselves from domination by the Church. Our history books so often give the impression that the Dark Ages were an unexplained misfortune that befell the human race (meaning Western Europe). Perhaps we should remind ourselves of the Theodosian Rule: Nicean belief (moving on to Roman Catholic belief) — good! Anybody else's belief — bad!

The ramblings of my last few paragraphs were intended to illustrate how the might of the Roman Empire faded, and was replaced by the might of the Roman Catholic Church and its bishops. This is a well-constructed story that has appeared in most of our history books ever since and it gives feelings of longevity, consistency and reliability. If you wanted to place your next life into the hands of a reliable authority, this was the way to go.

A point we need to remember is that every word of every book was written by human hand. Books were rare and precious. Books were also seen as powerful tools in the spread of religion, so if a man was considered to be in some way deviant, then his library was burnt! In today's world, a bit of book-burning is little more than a political gesture, they can be easily replaced. But in a world before printing, book-burning was a serious loss to the sum of human knowledge. Those in authority would burn the books of any opposition — a crude form of restricting belief. Another thought — how do you store your books? At a time when most royal households were itinerant, and common people lived in inflammable and mouse-ridden cottages, where could you store valuable books? Before the coming of universities, the only dry and solid buildings were the monasteries. (This may not be totally true, but you see the way my mind is working.) Part of the occupation of monks was writing: they produced copies of books. Thus, for the first thousand years of Christianity, most books were made by monks and stored in monasteries. Thus Church Authorities had close control over which writings survived and which didn't.

I have already mentioned the multitude of Christian heresies that were circulating in the third and fourth centuries (Chapter Five). We know their names and a quick sketch of their deviant beliefs as recorded by the Church, but we have little feel for the solidity of the people who followed these ideas, or for the number of people involved. It is all too easy to assume that they were all illiterate and not terribly bright, and therefore left us no records: or could it be that book-burning cleared away the evidence, with any surviving fragments ending their days on a monastic bonfire? Without any evidence at all, I have a suspicion that in the middle of the fifth century, as Roman military authority was falling apart, three quarters of Europe followed the simple and straightforward Arian version of Christianity, whilst only one quarter followed the Nicene doctrine that was central to what became the Roman Catholic Church. It is probably true that Arianism based itself on the simple style of life seen in the Bible, whereas the Roman church was about organisation with a big 'O'.

As a footnote, Roman military authority came to an official end with the Western insignia being sent to Byzantium, and the Dual Emperorship abolished in the year 480. Rome came under the control of Odoacer, the Germanic king of Italy, a good Christian, but of the Arian sort.

CHAPTER TEN
AND ON THROUGH THE DARK TOWARDS THE MIDDLE AGES

If Rome as a civil and military power came to an end in 480 — what next? We have already looked at the way the Roman Catholic Church was setting itself up to take over, but the world was getting wider and other forces were coming into play. That great centre of Christianity, Constantinople, or Byzantium, was getting ever more inward-looking. Furious debate raged as to whether you could, or could not; should, or should not, worship a painted image of a holy person. There was also a fear that men in government positions might devote their efforts to gaining personal wealth and passing it on to establish a family power base. The solution was to favour men who had had the operation — eunuchs! Thus we see a strange society in which there were three sexes. Constantinople became so engaged in its own affairs that it almost dropped out of world history — until Crusaders realised that here was a store of great wealth.

*****

North of the Alps, there was very little first-hand history in a largely illiterate world. A world of tribal hierarchy mixed with old pagan ideas and some newer Arian ones, all tempered by occasional discussions with the Pope over territorial rights. The year divided naturally into two parts, winter — and the fighting season. Franks fought Saxons or anybody else who got in their way. Success in battle brought booty; and with booty you could pay your soldiers and reward your supporters. Into this world, around 742, was born Charles, later to have the word 'Great' attached to his name: 'Charlemagne'.

Charles was of the royal line: his grandfather had led the forces that stopped the Muslim advance into France in 732 and he, himself, soon became military leader and the centre of government. He was firmly Christian, but a soldier by nature and did not allow his Christianity to get in the way of military or political necessity. He introduced laws against the looting of churches and the murder of priests but was not above slaughtering captives if it suited his objectives. These were indeed rough times!

As the time moved onward towards the Year of Our Lord 800, the 'known world' had taken on a new appearance. Rome had lost governmental control everywhere except for a small area around Rome itself, although it still claimed spiritual authority over the whole of Christendom. Byzantium held what we would now call Turkey, Greece and the Southern half of the Balkans, and was sunk in introspection and argument over the worship of idols. Not only that, but Byzantium had fallen into the hands of a woman! Starting off as Regent for her son, Irene gradually took over, eventually 'getting rid' of her son. She insisted on the title 'Emperor', but Charles and the Pope could not conceive of a woman in such a God-given position so there was a tacit assumption that the throne of Byzantium was vacant. Charles himself now ruled a substantial empire, one that stretched from the Bay of Biscay to the River Oder — France, Germany and lands to the south.

But, to use a currently fashionable phrase, we have not noticed 'the elephant in the room'. More than half of the Christian world had disappeared: lost to the extraordinarily rapid expansion of Islam. The west, the south and the east coasts of 'Our Sea', the Mediterranean, had fallen to this strange new religion. Spain, North Africa, Egypt, Palestine, Syria and out beyond the Caspian Sea, all lost to the Christian world. I feel tempted to add — without the religious centres of Rome and Byzantium noticing! Perhaps they were just glad to see the back of Alexandria, Antioch and Jerusalem, places where ideas sometimes differed from the cosy Catholicism of Rome.

There were thus three centres of Power in the remaining Christian World: the Pope in Rome, Charlemagne in his newly assembled Empire, and Byzantium, where the seat of power was vacant (Christian authority being unable to see a woman).

Pope Leo III faced a number of serious accusations and in 799 he was violently attacked with the apparent objective of striking out his eyes (a Byzantine method for rendering a person incapable of holding high office). Either the attack failed, or God repaired the damage; in either case, Leo went off to recover in Charlemagne's palace at Paderborn. At this point both centres of Christian authority were seen to have fallen upon hard times: both Rome and Byzantium had become places of decadence and violence. Was the Day of God's Judgement at hand? To add strength to this idea, stories circulated about the wealth, opulence and success of the new Muslim Court in Baghdad. There had clearly been ample opportunity for talks between Leo and Charles, but if records were made, none survive. Charles appears to have accepted the Pope's claim to be innocent of all the charges brought against him and Leo acknowledged Charles as Emperor of the Western Empire. At the Nativity Mass in St Peter's on Christmas Day 800, Leo placed a golden band upon Charles's head. From this point starts the concept of 'The Holy Roman Empire', with its Emperor crowned by God.

There is an obvious comparison to be made between Charlemagne and Constantine, in spite of the four hundred and seventy-five years separating them. Both were clearly involved in the blending together of the spiritual power of the Christian Church with the material strength and the needs of the State, but I see a distinct difference. Constantine had known what he was doing: he gathered together the wayward parts of the Christian Church, helped them to a central theme and fitted them into his system of government. Whereas Charlemagne had the mind of a soldier: he made a good Emperor, but the subtleties of religious politics were a bit beyond him. He could never get on with Nicean thinking, and dismissed it as 'The Synod of the Greeks'. Pope Leo, on the other hand, saw the grand ceremony on Christmas Day as a way of securing permanent military protection for the Church and also of distracting the public mind away from his dodgy past. Charlemagne seems to have been somewhat taken by surprise and he left the Christmas ceremony wondering what to do next.

AND ON THROUGH THE DARK TOWARDS THE MIDDLE AGES

*****

There is a book sub-titled 'A History of the World through Islamic Eyes' by Tamim Ansary which introduces an idea that is new to me. He sees the world of the Mediterranean and Western Europe as the land where transport takes place by water: he sees the lands to the East as places where transport is done overland (with China and India lying out beyond). He notes an area of stress where these two worlds come into contact (think of Palestine). Was it by chance that Christianity arose in this area of stress? We might also like to note that Rome lies safely in the world of water transport.

It is of course a bit nationalistic to refer to 'The East' or to 'The Middle East' because I am sure that the people who live there see themselves as living at the centre of the known world. However, I shall make my apologies and move on.

For a thousand years and more, people in the Middle East (Persia) followed a religion called Zoroastrianism, a fairly straightforward dualistic belief coming from the teaching of Zoroaster, who seems to have lived at much the same time as Solomon and King David (the Bronze age of a thousand BC). It is Zoroastrianism that gives us the words 'Magus' and 'Magi' for the priests who turn up at the Christian Nativity scene. Then in the seventh century AD, at a desert trading centre in Arabia there started an idea that was to shake the whole world (and still does!). In broad outline, a man called Mohammed spent time in meditation in a cave. The details are a little unclear, but a teaching came from God, through Mohammed, and was set down in a Book, The Koran. This Book and the guidance of Mohammed became the centre of a new religion, Islam.

Mohammed began to teach that there was only one God (not the multitude that were currently being worshipped in Mecca) and that to seek your own salvation, you had to follow God's rules. Many of these rules were close to what a good Christian would aspire to: like leading a good life, avoiding drunkenness and violence and helping the poor and the weak. Unfortunately, these rules did not suit the rich men of Mecca who enjoyed, and made money from, drinking, gambling and prostitution. So a plan was devised to murder Mohammed. Mohammed and his supporters got wind of the plot and so left Mecca, travelling northward to the town of Yathrib where, in due course, Mohammed was accepted as a leading citizen and as the arbitrator bringing Muslim peace between prickly local tribes. Success led the town to change its name to 'The City' (Meaning the City of the Prophet), 'Medina' in the Arab language. This move by Mohammed and his supporters from Mecca to Medina (known as the 'Hegira') was seen to mark the expansion of the Muslim Faith from a man's effort to follow the word of God; to the wider duty placed on a man to respect and support other Muslims. Islam had become a community Faith. In his book, 'Destiny Disrupted', Tamim Ansary writes,

> "— Islam presents a plan for building a righteous community. Individuals earn their place in heaven by participating as members of that community and engaging in the Islamic social project, which is to build a world in which orphans won't feel abandoned and in which widows won't ever be homeless, hungry, or afraid." The struggle to achieve such a world was called 'Jihad'.

Mohammed had become an orphan at the age of six and had been taken in by his grandfather. The grandfather died, and Mohammed moved on to the house of an uncle. Some while later this uncle had a son of his own who grew up seeing Mohammed as his elder brother (although, technically, they were cousins). In due course this son, Ali, married Mohammed's daughter, and because Mohammed had no sons, Ali came to be regarded as Mohammed's closest relative and natural heir. Mohammed had made it clear in his teaching that he was the last of God's Messengers, so when he died in the year 11 AH (eleven years after the Hegira) there was consternation — no one had given thought to what should happen next. You can't, after all, elect the next saint! But they did need a leader. Ali was a very obvious candidate: he had a lifelong association with The Prophet and was father to Mohammed's grandsons, but there were older, more experienced men who had worked with Mohammed on setting up the new society and Arabs have a great respect for age. It is a sad fact that within hours of The Prophet's death a division began to appear in the One Community of Islam; one group believed that leadership should follow the blood line through Ali (those who became Shi'a Muslims) and the other group believed a leader should be elected, or selected, from the best men available, (going on to become Sunni Muslims). The word 'best' is important in this context: one suspects that in later days, 'best' came to mean the man most likely to expand the empire and increase its wealth. Both groups were of course firm followers of Mohammed and The Koran, but the Sunni kept a firm eye on the material world: the Shi'a had more concern for spiritual matters. This division became set in stone with the murder and decapitation of Hussein, son of Ali, grandson of Mohammed. To the Shi'a, Hussein took on something of the aura that Christians see in Christ, and beheading became a religiously significant form of execution.

<u>Key Dates put onto the Christian Calendar</u>

Birth of Mohammed	around	570
The Hegira		622
Death of Mohammed		632
The first four successors followed by: -		
Start of the Umayyad Empire		661
Murder of Hussein		680
Muslim forces move into Western Europe (Spain)		711

But the question that still rises in the minds of western historians is, "How did the Muslim Faith take over so much territory so quickly?" A Muslim would no doubt put it all down to the Will of Allah. (As a footnote it is worth mentioning that Allah is, in fact, two words: Al — The: Lah — God. Therefore, to say "THE GOD" is to make it clear that there is only one God, and not three!) The material reasons for Muslim success can be argued over, but a few factors clearly played a part. There was enthusiasm for a new religion, when compared with the rather old and tired religions that had worn themselves out arguing about heresy. In Islam, all men were equal — and women were only a little way behind. The Koran could only be properly read in Arabic, so Arabic became the common language across a vast empire with resulting improvements in trade. (Compare the Christian Church's attachment to Latin.) And finally, Muslims saw the importance of tax: there was a tax paid by Muslims for the support of 'the Islamic social project', and there was a tax paid by non-Muslims for being non-Muslims.

*****

In mainland Europe Charlemagne had been working toward the reconstruction of an ordered Roman-style empire, with a strong Christian presence, and although he himself was barely literate, he was trying to revive an interest in the 'classics' of Greece and Rome. At this point we need to remind ourselves that four hundred years earlier, Christians under Theodosius had done their best to destroy this 'classical' material because it was seen to pre-date Nicean Christianity and was therefore worthless, and a distraction. (Recent news broadcasts have told a parallel story of Muslim extremists blowing up monuments that dated before Mohammed for exactly the same reason!) Charles died in 814 and his empire suffered many divisions among his children and grandchildren, until the 850's when Charlemagne's Empire can be said to have drifted out of existence.

The end of the eighth century and into the ninth had seen not only the growth of Charlemagne's Empire; it also saw the terror of the Vikings. Let me explain. As the climate softened and the last Ice Age drew to a close, people moved north to exploit the newly available space. It is in the nature of things that the men who led this advance northward were a pretty rough bunch, doing whatever was necessary for their personal survival. Then think of Norway: very little land suitable for cultivation; but a lot of fish. Again, the aggressive geography of the Norwegian coast meant that roads or tracks to link one settlement to the next were difficult or impossible. Two good reasons to develop boats! Somewhere around the eighth century AD a flash of genius lighted up these people. We can imagine that, up to that time, boats had been the practical everyday sort, good for a day's fishing, or for a trip to a neighbouring island to visit relatives: and then the flash! Boats became symbols of power, big enough and seaworthy enough to transport a fighting band along with the stores necessary to keep them going for a week or more. The seas had become their highway. Their life of trading dried fish and reindeer products was no longer important; they could go out a-raiding. Their gods led them to religious houses conveniently close to the sea, or on the banks of navigable rivers, each house well supplied with gold and silver, and guarded only by old men. The men were easily killed and the women raped. Thus, if they should come that way again in twenty years' time, the young men would all carry Viking blood in their veins. With generous supplies of gold and silver, slaves could be bought to do the common work, and the Vikings became a fighting aristocracy.

AND ON THROUGH THE DARK TOWARDS THE MIDDLE AGES

The most complete surviving Viking warship (The Oseberg Ship)

The Vikings had a well-constructed belief system. They saw themselves as living in the middle of the world (Midgard) with dwellings for the gods at its centre (Asgard). At the centre of Asgard grew the World Tree (Yggdrasill) with its top reaching the sky and its three roots encompassing the whole world: the world where people live; the world of the giants, and the 'Otherworld'. Outside Midgard lay the dangerous wilderness where there were more giants. Battle between gods and giants would eventually bring this world to an end, 'Ragnarok' (the extinction of the gods) after which, perhaps, the sons of the gods might start a new world under a new World Tree.

It is clear that the one thing on the mind of early Vikings was treasure: gold and silver. They didn't give a damn about works of art, it was the precious metal they wanted, and if men stood in their way, then they would be killed without a second thought. The Vikings were physically strong (for they were rowing sea-going ships) and their religion taught them aggression. Add to this the absence of any form of communication; no forewarnings, the first sign you might have of a Viking raid is when they smash down your door. Vikings spread fear along the coasts — and then along the navigable rivers. You might reasonably ask why these young and virile Viking warriors in pursuit of rape and pillage would choose to raid a monastery full of elderly men living in poverty? Perhaps all is not as it seems! The 'elderly men' idea may have been true, and thus the Vikings could expect little serious opposition, but the vow of poverty was a personal thing for the monks themselves: it did not extend to the buildings in which they lived. Almost without meaning to, monasteries had become storehouses of wealth. A rich man might see a donation to a monastery as an investment in his own afterlife or, again, a monastery could be seen as a strong building full of honourable men: a sort of bank deposit box; somewhere to leave your family treasure whilst you went off fighting in another part of the country.

There is a case for seeing the Norway-based Vikings moving west and south, taking over the sparsely populated Shetland Islands, the Orkneys and Iceland; then the Isle of Man and setting up a slaving station in a place that was to become Dublin; expanding to the rivers of France before moving on into the Mediterranean, and taking over Sicily. The Sweden-based Vikings seem to have gone east, trading their way along Russian rivers, eventually reaching Byzantium. The Danish Vikings seem to have been less addicted to travel: they came and took over the eastern part of England.

In England, the early Viking technique of the lightning raid was soon to expand into a more orthodox military invasion. Danes were over-wintering in East Anglia by the 850's and before long their 'Great Heathen Army' was rampaging up and down the country. King Alfred earned his place in history by gaining some sort of control over the Danish hordes and restricting them to East Anglia and Northumbria, land that came to be called 'The Danelaw'. The time of King Alfred was a time of revival in Christian belief. (Perhaps as an offshoot of Charlemagne's recent efforts to renew enthusiasm for Christianity.) In any case the Danish incursions

AND ON THROUGH THE DARK TOWARDS THE MIDDLE AGES

were seen by some as a punishment from God on an England that had lost its spiritual way. One method used in an attempt to persuade the Danes into a civilised way of life was to give them money: fairly regular payments that came to be called 'The Danegelt'. For example, one such payment was for 16,000 pounds. This was not, of course, a neat bundle of £50 notes: it was probably 16,000 pounds in weight of silver — seven tons, perhaps ten cartloads! As time went on, armies got bigger, and the required payments got bigger: 48,000 pounds in 1012 and a vast 82,500 pounds in 1018. (37 tons!) What happened to all this wealth? Well, some of it has been dug up in Scandinavia, but I have little doubt that the bulk was melted down and recycled.

We are of course still in the Dark Ages and we have very little by way of background information. We have no real idea of the actual relationship between Englishman and Dane, either at the personal, or at government level. For what it is worth, place names in the eastern half of England still carry a hint of Scandinavian language. So, did the Danes get back into their boats and quietly row away? Or did they simply adopt Christianity and blend into their surroundings? We hear of St Brice's Day Massacre (1002) when the King (Aethelred the Unready) ordered all Danish men in England to be slain! Presumably in response to some perceived threat. It is very unclear how many, if any, were killed under this order. We do know that back in 927 King Athelstan had announced that England was now one unified and Christian community. (We also know that ninety years after that, the whole of England was under the control of a Danish King — Canute, son of Swein Forkbeard!) It is all very confusing!

The Vikings from Sweden seem to have sailed east across the Baltic, past the marshlands where St Petersburg now stands, and on into the Russian river system. They became known as 'The Rus'. But whether they gave their name to Russia, or whether it was the other way round, is a bit unclear. I have a feeling that around the year 900, in the lands to the north of the Black Sea, changes were already beginning to happen with improvements in agriculture and a reduction in inter-tribal warfare. Into this scene came the Rus. Before long, trade routes were established up and down the country, from Novgorod to Kiev and the native tribes were paying tribute (tax) to the Rus. It was not long before the Rus were making the trip down the Dnieper and across the Black Sea to Byzantium, where the usual trade goods of furs, walrus ivory (known as fish teeth) and slaves could be expanded to the silks and spices of the East. Journeys down the Volga and across the Caspian Sea to Baghdad were also possible where the Abbasid Empire seemed to have unlimited supplies of silver.

In his book 'Vikings', Neil Oliver tells of Rus traders being mightily impressed with Byzantium and, no doubt, wishing to get involved in a process that could generate such wealth. Back in Kiev, the Rus Prince Vladimir (978-1015) decided to abandon pagan beliefs and move forward. His agents reported that they found no joy among Jews, or the Muslims so, guided by the splendour, beauty and opulence of Byzantium, the Rus became Orthodox Christians (989).

(Are we, perhaps, being led towards an idea that links Vikings: Money; and Christianity?)

I have attempted a quick sketch of Danish Vikings in Eastern England, and another of Swedish Vikings in Kiev, so I now want to complete the Scandinavian trio by looking at Norwegian Vikings as they affected the north western corner of mainland Europe. It is roughly true to say that the peoples who lived in what we would now call the Netherlands and North Germany were descended from the forest dwellers that the Romans had failed to conquer. By the later years of the eighth century and into the ninth there was a fairly restless population of Saxons, Franks and Danes (yes, them again) together with a number of lesser-known tribes all making some sort of a living out of agriculture, production and trade. A money economy was beginning to take shape based on the silver penny (or denier, from denarius), and trade based on silver coins was proving to be so much quicker and easier than barter. Also easier was theft, and of course, debt. We might think of a collection of tribal groups constantly nudging and tweaking their neighbours, taking tolls on passing trade goods and occasionally taking a prisoner who would be released only after a suitable bag of silver coin had changed hands. Into this restless country came Charlemagne's ideas of an orderly empire that was coupled with an increasing devotion to the Christian faith as seen through the eyes of the Pope in Rome. How much effect did Charlemagne's ideas have? My immediate response would be, 'Not a lot' although others might differ. Christian thinking may have done something to tidy up social organisation, the "See you in Church next Sunday" sort of thing. But whether there was any serious increase in Christian understanding and morality seems unlikely, although there does seem to have been a 'pulling up of the socks' in the monasteries. (Monasteries in Charlemagne's empire had been instructed to follow the Rule of Saint Benedict in 816.)

Into this world came the 'Northmen', the Vikings from Norway. They came first as traders taking a place in established trading centres and having a keen eye on the silver coinage, then becoming something of a mixture between trader and warlord. They were looking for some land of their own. Elbowing their way into a patch of land, they were no doubt told that, following Charlemagne's Christianising rules, land could only be held by Christians. So they became Christians! The Northmen had become Normans in Normandy.

That might be seen as the 'traders' version of the story, but there is another, the 'raiders' version.

Into the Frankish world came the 'Northmen', as usual looking for treasure. They would raid and take all the portable wealth they could find or, if the opportunity was offered, they would accept a payment for not raiding. A sentence in Janet L. Nelson's contribution to 'The Vikings' paints a clear picture. "Nothing was left unscathed in Quentovic (a port near Boulogne) except for those buildings which the Northmen were paid to spare." You could hire a band of Northmen to protect you and your interests against attacks by other Northmen, but there was a slight catch. Following the

AND ON THROUGH THE DARK TOWARDS THE MIDDLE AGES

Charlemagne Rules, you could only hire such a band if they were Christians — fortunately these Viking Northmen found no difficulty in saying that they were Christians, particularly if there was a payment involved. Through the later part of the ninth century, Viking bands ranged widely along both sides of the English Channel looking for plunder. However, they soon learned to avoid Wessex where King Alfred had set up an effective network of thirty bank and ditch earthwork castles, some of which can be seen to this day (Try Wallingford).

So we come to 911 when the King of the West Franks granted Rouen and some of the surrounding country to a Viking leader called Rollo in the hope that his men would become a block on the River Seine preventing other raiders penetrating up into the area around Paris. Rollo's great, great, great grandson is known to us as William the Conqueror!

So, one part of the Viking World had given up ranging the high seas in search of treasure, and settled on fertile land in Northern France where they adopted the local language and spent the next hundred and fifty-five years (911-1066) becoming the Duchy of Normandy. It is worth reminding ourselves at this point that the Viking interest in money had led them to raid monasteries — and the only places where records were written and stored were — in monasteries. So Vikings were guaranteed a bad press! However, there was one aspect of Viking invasion that deserves our admiration. They could move into a country and take over control; pick up the dropped threads of the previous government and in the space of a very few years, everyone forgot they were invaders. To move into a new country and blend in as a worker is one thing: to blend in and become the boss is clever!

By the tenth century, Charlemagne's efforts to re-form an orderly European empire had fallen to pieces, and we were back in the world of competing tribes. However, Charlemagne's efforts in conjunction with Pope Leo to put energy into the Christian Church had proved a little more successful and much of mainland Europe was now being guided by a firmly Rome-based religion. (I do wonder if this was the point at which the old Arian Christianity was finally swept away.) Was it, perhaps, this move to organise the whole of Christendom from one central point that drew attention to costs. Costs associated with travel and transport, more staff, more buildings and longer delays. To meet rising costs, Rome needed a rising income. The Vikings knew about money and were always interested in power — perhaps an unlikely partnership could be arranged?

It is interesting that this period of development for the Vikings in Normandy (911-1066) coincides almost exactly with a period in Rome that is politely described as "a low period for the Papacy" from 896 to 1049.

This low period starts with the death of Pope Formosus on 4th April 896. He was buried: then, after a while, dug up, dressed, sat on a throne and a formal trial took place to judge his handling of a fairly obscure part of ecclesiastical procedure. He was found guilty, stripped and thrown into the Tiber. A later Pope, Theodore II, recovered the body from the river (?). No other Popes could quite match this for drama, but a few were thrown into prison, where they were quietly strangled. (Presumably to avoid the spilling of blood!) There was a great deal of corruption with strong commercial interests involved and some of the Popes were appointed with no other object than to look after their patron's commercial interests. Given this situation, it is not surprising that some Popes had very little religious knowledge or interest. Presumably to enhance their qualifications, some were said to be the sons of priests or bishops and Pope John XI was thought to be a son of Pope Sergius III! (All very different from the papacy of a thousand years later.) Among the forty-odd Popes of this period, a few made efforts to break with this degenerate pattern and turn the attention of the Papacy back to Church and Monastery, but none were strong enough for the job until The Holy Roman Emperor, Henry III moved in and formally deposed three Popes whose positions were unclear, Benedict IX, Sylvester III and Gregory VI. (As a footnote, it is interesting to mention that Benedict IX had been made Pope when he was only twenty years old and had no religious training or interest. He was described as 'dissolute'. He was deposed three times, but on two occasions managed to claw his way back with large sums of money involved. If the Office of Pope is thought to stretch from St Peter to the present day in an unbroken chain, then Benedict IX is one of the links — sorry, Catholics!) Benedict was finally deposed on 16th July 1048. Then the following year Pope Leo IX was elected and he started the clean-up campaign in earnest. Among the first strands of the clean-up was an order enforcing celibacy on all clergy.

With our attention taken by the Papacy, and by developments in Normandy, we should not forget that some of the Viking Sea Raiders were still in business. Raiding armies with origins back in Denmark and Norway were still on the lookout for plunder and for lands to conquer. King Aethelred paid money to the Northmen to go away, in order to give England time to build up land and sea defences; only to discover that after the payment, there was not enough money left to carry out the work. Aethelred went through this sequence a number of times and this is one of the reasons why Aethelred came to be called 'The Unready'. Many of our older history books have looked for a more charitable meaning for the label 'The Unready'. Perhaps someone who ruled without proper guidance from a council? Unfortunately, I think his label was all too accurate: Aethelred was indeed, unready! He was a poor judge of situations, either political or military, and he made poor decisions that failed to reach obvious objectives, and he upset important people along the way. It was Fate that determined that Dodgy King Aethelred was on the throne for the unusually long period of thirty-eight years (978-1016).

This period of Aethelred's reign saw a couple of important changes within the world of the Vikings. The Vikings had of course been the major threat to England for two hundred years, but somewhere around the year 1000 the Vikings adopted Christianity and met up with the stress and worry among many Christians who thought that the world would be coming to an end in the year 1000 (The Christian Ragnarok!). There was also development in the internal organisation among Viking groups. We have already seen how Viking settlers in Northern France were converting themselves into the Duchy of Normandy; the homelands of Norway and Denmark were also changing. No more the drunken feasting commemorated in 'Beowolf' (belief is optional!). Both Norway and Denmark, and Sweden as well, were developing themselves into kingdoms, with a hierarchy of nobles, a structure and an aristocracy. A Viking raid was no longer twenty men with axes: it was a hundred ships lying offshore waiting to be paid tons of silver to go away, or else they would come and take over your country! This is, of course, an imagined scenario, but you get the idea: a new situation sometimes called the Second Viking Age. If it gave any comfort, England is now being attacked by Christians! (The last pagan Viking settlement in England had been expelled from York in 954.)

Over a number of years, a largely Danish army under Thorkell the Tall was progressively successful in taking over England until, towards the end of 1013, Thorkell escorted Aethelred and his family to the Court in Normandy for their own safety. Swein Forkbeard, a leading power in the invasion, became, in effect, king, but died a couple of months later. His teenage son, Canute, was judged to be a bit young, so Aethelred was brought back for a couple of years to fill in, then in 1016, Canute became king and, followed by two of his sons, England was under a Danish (or, if you prefer it, a Viking) King for twenty-six years before reverting to a son of Dodgy Aethelred, Edward the Confessor.

CHAPTER ELEVEN
A TIME OF CHANGE

From the first Viking raid on Lindisfarne in 793, and on through most of the ninth century, monasteries had been under attack. It seems reasonable to assume that the English Anglo-Saxon man of the day was disappointed that God had failed to defend his principal agents. Not only that, but the thieves were enjoying their loot! English Christians had a lot to think about.

Once upon a time there had been a thin sprinkling of monasteries out in the wilder parts of England and in the adjacent lands. These monasteries and their monks had two fundamental purposes. Firstly, to study works of Christian heritage and to get closer to God; to conserve and copy books and to teach all who came seeking to their door. Their second purpose was to allow a spiritual atmosphere, channelled through themselves to enlighten all people: a small spoonful of Christian yeast to make the whole country rise. And then much of this world was to fade away under the onslaught of treasure-hungry Vikings, leaving Christians confused. Where was God?

At this point it is important to mention a subtle change that was just beginning to stir in England. This change was so essentially subtle that mention of dates may seem inappropriate but, in order to draw your mind to the right sort of area, think of 950. The change I have in mind is the change from an oral tradition to a world of written record. Reading and writing began to have an impact on people — not of course that everyone was literate — we had to wait another nine hundred years for that — but if King or Council made a decision, it would be written down, and if questioned it could be read out again years later. (And historians begin to have dependable sources.) In a land of oral tradition there had been little to separate history from romance and both were vulnerable to the death of a storyteller. Could the revival of Charlemagne's ideas of organised Christianity be turning occasional visits to a monastery into regular visits to a church? Just a thought.

These visits to a monastery, or to the grave of a saint, or to the grave of a martyr, had been an important part in the life of any active Christian for a very long time. Indeed, the idea of a group gathering around the tomb of a martyr is a strong reminder of the first two hundred years of Christianity, before there were churches. (I am reminded that back in the 1950's I visited Lourdes and saw the collections of crutches left behind by those granted a miraculous cure. So something of the old idea of a journey to a special place — and a reward — is still with us.)

'Saint Dunstan' is a name well known from its modern use in charity fundraising, but the original was active in the middle years of the tenth century, first at Glastonbury and then as Archbishop of Canterbury. Dunstan did much to bring system and order back into monastic life. Dunstan and King Edgar (959-975) set about church reform, in part repairing the damage remaining from the Viking raids of the previous century, and in part taking up Cluniac ideas that were coming in from the other side of the channel. This was a time of great interest in relics, and in the burial places of saints and martyrs. Books were prepared listing the miracle cures attributed to each saint and his relics, and visits to Rome became popular because that was seen as a source for more relics. Church interiors were readjusted to make access to reliquaries more convenient and Saint Swithin was dug up from his chosen burial place and moved inside the church. (At Canterbury a number of cures were achieved by a flask containing the water that had been used to wash Saint Dunstan's stick!) Much work was undertaken to encourage visitors (and fill the collecting boxes) while attempting to preserve a proper sense of dignity and mystery. On a slightly more serious note, men and women were still travelling to celebrated religious houses in search of spiritual instruction. (Women at this date had a degree of freedom that they were to lose under the Normans.)

Casting our minds back to Chapter Ten, there was some mention of the 'low period for the Papacy' and Dunstan's time sits well within these dates. Dunstan was made Archbishop of Canterbury in 960 and went off to Rome to receive a pallium from the Pope. Four

A TIME OF CHANGE

years later this Pope, John XII, died from a stroke whilst in bed with a married woman, (an alternative story had him strangled by an enraged husband). This was indeed a low period for the Papacy.

This period from 950 to 1066 is worthy of more attention that it is usually given. It covers significant changes to the way in which the Christian religion was observed. It was also the time when political vision was getting wider: organisations were getting larger; what had been raiding parties were turning themselves into nations, and England had recently changed itself into one united kingdom out of Wessex, Mercia and the rest. The age-old Anglo-Saxon ideas of an essentially monastic Christianity were being overtaken by the sort of Church Organisation that can look the Political Government squarely in the eye. Starting, perhaps, with an idea from Pope Leo III and Charlemagne; on to the teachings in the Abbey at Cluny, then to Dunstan, and on to King Canute who staged his well-known demonstration. (For those unfamiliar with the story: Canute sat on the beach and commanded the incoming tide to go back — it didn't. Thus the tide was seen to follow God's law, not the King's command.) The story may or may not be true, but the message was clear: God, and by association His Church, rank above the Kings of this world.

The foundations were being laid upon which the Norman invaders would build a new world.

As a footnote: - in 1050 Edward the Confessor made a start on building a Benedictine Abbey beside the Thames at Westminster. (Following the French tradition rather than the ancient Anglo-Saxon idea of a monastery.) He chose a dry patch of ground known as Thorney Island and those of you with a taste for red herring may like to note the Encyclopaedia Britannica suggestion that this Thorney Island had once held a very ancient church founded by King Lucius — see the essay on Augustine.

CHAPTER TWELVE
ENGLAND'S MOST IMPORTANT DAY

As the time had moved onward into the 1050's and 1060's, there was much interest in what was likely to happen when England's King, Edward the Confessor, died. Under Anglo-Saxon law there was little doubt; the next king would be the one chosen by the Witan, or Council. Unfortunately, some of the claimants had no knowledge of or interest in Anglo-Saxon law. There were, perhaps half a dozen plausible claimants but only two need concern us here. One was Harald Hardrada, King of Norway, a giant of a man who had once been the commander of the Varangian Guard, a largely Viking-staffed police force based in Byzantium; the other was William, Duke of Normandy. Both, you might note, with strong Viking roots. There is little doubt that in the 1060's William, Duke of Normandy, was the strong man of Europe. He had position and power and intelligence in both the military and in the political sense and he seems to have convinced Pope Alexander II that he was the true heir to Charlemagne, spreading a firmly Rome-based Christianity across Europe. (Go back a few pages and you may note that the Papacy itself had come back to life in 1049, only a few years before.) The Pope sent William a banner and gave a papal blessing to the invasion of England. Alexander clearly saw England as being in need of some religious correction. (Incidentally, Alexander had done his training at Bec in Normandy, working under Lanfranc, who became William's archbishop.)

Events were triggered by the death of Edward the Confessor on 5th January 1066: on his deathbed he had acknowledged Harold Godwinson as his successor and at dawn the next day he was buried in Westminster Abbey. (Which had been completed and consecrated only eight days before!) Later in the same day, Harold was elected by the Witan and he went on to be enthroned at a High Mass in the Abbey. (A busy day! Readers of detective fiction may find they have questions to ask, although it must be said that Edward was in his early or middle sixties, a not uncommon age to die at this period. It might also be said that Edward was a devoted churchman who saw the building of Westminster Abbey as his life's work — and that work was now complete.) As the news spread, those who felt they had some claim to the English throne began to stir. With hindsight, it seems clear that Edward had exploited his childlessness as a political tool, and had made promises of the succession in a number of directions.

First to move was Harald Hardrada, coming down from Norway, assembling his forces in Orkney and moving on into the Humber estuary (having burnt Scarborough on the way — old habits die hard!). They left their ships and made their way towards York. At Fulford, two miles south of the town, the army of Harald met the army of the Northern Earls. Total victory for Harald H, 'with great slaughter!' In the following days, Harald was no doubt patting himself on the back and waiting for the formal surrender of York into his hands, along with more portable prizes. He was jolted out of these thoughts when he met up with a different army at Stamford Bridge, five miles east of York: the army of Harold Godwinson. Total victory for Harold G, 'with great slaughter!' Harald H is killed. Three days later and two hundred and twenty odd miles away, William, Duke of Normandy landed on English soil. I think we can safely assume that William had some knowledge of Harald Hardrada's plans: it was unlikely to have been coincidence.

So, in the nineteen days that followed winning one of the Great Battles of the mediaeval world, Harold G and his men had to ride or walk two hundred and twenty miles to face a second 'Great Battle of the mediaeval world'. As we all know, they lost — but it was a damn close thing! As the sun went down on 14th October, England faced a very different future: England had seen its most important day!

ENGLAND'S MOST IMPORTANT DAY

Key dates within 1066

5th January	Edward the Confessor dies.
6th January	Harold Godwinson crowned.
18th September	Harald Hardrada and his army land on English soil.
20th September	Harald H fights the Northern Earls at Fulford and wins.
25th September	Harald H surprised by the arrival of an army under Harold Godwinson. They fight at Stamford Bridge and Harold G wins. Harald H dies.
28th September	William's forces land at Pevensey.
14th October	The Battle of Hastings, Harold G dies.
25th December	William crowned at Westminster Abbey.

(As a very small footnote, before we weep over the destruction of an ancient Anglo-Saxon kingdom by Viking Norman savagery, let us remember that intermarriage among top people has always been a power to mix things up. Harold Godwinson's mother was called Gytha Thorkelsdottir, and you can't get more Viking than that!)

Not long after the Norman invasion there seems to have been some effort to include a few Anglo-Saxons in the running of the country, but this idea was quickly abandoned and from here on England was ruled by French-speaking Normans: sheep became mutton and cows became beef. The Normans were true sons of their Viking forbears and showed a clear interest in land and money. The land and portable wealth of any Anglo-Saxon who had fought against William now became William's property by right of conquest. Any Anglo-Saxon who had maintained a low profile and avoided the fighting was deemed to have submitted to William, and by this submission his land also became William's property.

However, William could be generous, and he allowed the non-combatant Anglo-Saxons to buy back their submitted lands for an appropriate price. The land belonged to the Normans, and William parcelled it out among the men who had helped him to victory. I have little doubt that these newly enriched Norman lords saw the Anglo-Saxon peasants as a lower form of life with traditions and buildings of no value. The villages of the southern corn lands were important because that was where the slaves lived (sorry, I forgot: 'peasants'). But their churches were scruffy and mostly of wood — intolerable for a rich Norman lord with a new enthusiasm for the Church of Rome. A village church needed to be a dominating feature, a centre for village organisation, a place where the teaching of Rome could be delivered to everyone and where the tithes and other monies could be gathered in. The quieter, more reflective ways of the old Saxon Church were swept away, along with their buildings. Christian ideas that went back six hundred years or more had to be toughened up to suit the new Norman world.

It is now time to come back to the main theme of this book. How do we relate the newly tidied up Roman Christianity that the Pope clearly thought William was bringing to England, with the violence and brutality that mark out the early part of William's reign? It is, perhaps, easy to account for the violence. William and around seven thousand men were taking over a country of two or three million people: it was an illiterate world that had not heard of newspapers or television, so news spread by word of mouth, and nothing spreads faster than news of spectacular violence. The Lords of land north of the Humber had always felt themselves to be far enough away from London and the south to run things in their own way and the first few years after the Conquest saw Northern Earls flexing their muscles and having quiet words with the King of Denmark. Around 1070, William decided it was time for a final solution and launched a campaign that came to be called 'The Harrying of the North'. The land, from York to Durham, was devastated: every human being and every animal killed; every building and every store of food or seed corn burnt. The north became a wasteland. Resistance to William faded away.

So what of Christianity? With a man like William in charge, there was little doubt that Christianity would take on the form William wanted: and what William wanted was an extension to the world of northern France, with large and impressive churches, together with monasteries following the rule of St Benedict: all bearing echoes from the time of Charlemagne and his partnership with Pope Leo in Rome; and all working easily with William and his new government. (Memories of Constantine come to mind.)

*****

Before we launch ourselves into the land where 'English History Really Begins', let us have a brief review of Christianity in England before 1066.

More than eight hundred years ago, somewhere around the year 251, Alban had been executed for being a Christian. (A name still familiar to us as the town of St Albans.) In 314, the new Roman Emperor Constantine, with his enthusiasm for Christianity, called a Council at Arles in southern Gaul and three English (British) bishops travelled to attend. England was, of course, still the Roman Province of Britannia and somewhere around 350 a mosaic floor showing a head of Christ was constructed in Dorset. In the early 400's there was something of an argument between the British monk Pelagius and Saint Jerome (the one who wrote the Bible) over the spiritual capabilities that might exist within a Christian individual. In 430 Palladius* was sent to Ireland, and Germain to Britain, by Pope Celestine. Not so much to introduce Christianity — more to 'correct' the Christianity that was already here! My suspicion is that 'what was here' was Christianity with an

Footnote: Do not confuse Pelagius with Palladius — they are very different people.)

Alexandrian flavour with an emphasis on monastic life and solitary prayer. Celestine, on the other hand, had been influenced by the political/religious mix of Bishop Ambrose, and by the out and out religious theology of Bishop Augustine of Hippo, not to mention the rank intolerance he must have inherited from the Roman Emperor Theodosius (died 395). Irish monks may have seen Rome's politico-religious drive to encompass the whole world as irrelevant to their ambition to live with God at a personal level. (Alexandria and Rome were to split apart and go their separate ways a few years later, at the Council of Chalcedon in 451.) As a footnote: - Palladius died, and his place was taken by Saint Patrick. Could it be that Patrick found himself facing two varieties of Christianity: having to follow two different paths at the same time? Is this, perhaps, a key to Irish history? It might be around this date of 430 that Ninian started to set up a school/monastery in south west Scotland, to be followed a couple of generations later by Illtud in south Wales. In the 540's Columba was studying in Ireland before setting up on Iona, and it was from Iona that the Irish monk Aiden went on to found Lindisfarne in 635. (One might almost say that the spread and development of Christianity in England was proceeding very nicely and hardly noticed the arrival of Rome's representative, Augustine, in 597.) In the early 600's there was something of a surge of invaders from mainland Europe, people usually called Anglo-Saxons, who are often referred to as 'pagans'. But I have a suspicion that some may have brought with them the old Arian form of Christian belief. (Any hint of Arian belief was carefully ignored and rubbed out of Roman records.) Then, Rome's superior administration (and Peter holding the keys to Heaven) led to a vote in favour of Rome at the Synod of Whitby in 664, although some groups took many years before they fell into line. It is noteworthy that the Synod of Whitby happened very soon after the world-shattering expansion of Islamic faith in the 640's and the 650's. Nothing was said!

Was the loss of two-thirds of the Christian lands not worth a mention? Was the timing of the Synod just a coincidence?

793 THE START OF THE VIKING DISASTER

Vikings discover the riches held in monasteries. Most monasteries raided, some many times. Many monks killed. Many monasteries abandoned. (Refer back to Chapter Eleven). Attempts to make good the spiritual loss saw the import of ideas from mainland Europe: echoes from the attempts to revive Charlemagne's Holy Roman Empire; and ideas of religious discipline coming in from the Abbey at Cluny. We can speculate that the Anglo-Saxon 'man in the street' was deeply unhappy: his Christian religion, centred on the monasteries — ancient beyond all measure — perhaps even contiguous with life in the Bible — had not only been shattered by the Vikings, but what was left was now being replaced by foreign ideas — ideas in a foreign language, and ideas that seemed to centre on Rome rather than Jerusalem.

Before 793 — a whiff of desert hermitages.

After 1066 — Power, discipline, and behind many a locked door — a pile of money.

CHAPTER THIRTEEN
THE CHURCH IN NORMAN ENGLAND AND ON INTO THE PLANTAGENETS (1066 to 1399)

It needs to be emphasised from the start that the monasteries raided by the Vikings in the ninth century were very different places from the monasteries built by the 'sons of the Vikings' two hundred and fifty years later: different in physical form, and different in theological objectives. The 'Celtic Saints' as they are sometimes called, had needed isolation and independence for their study and worship. The monasteries of Norman foundation were very different. They were bigger and involved many more people: they were built in or near a town and had an architectural presence. Growing up to a hundred or more monks and a similar number of lay brothers, together with builders and assorted support workers, along with the workers' families, there were a lot of people involved, with an obvious requirement for water and food supplies, not to mention sewage disposal. Commercial development grew up at the monastery gate in much the same way as a civilian vicus grew up at the entrance to a Roman military fort. So, we have a very different picture for a Norman monastery, even before we mention religion. The Celtic Saints had occupied land that no one else wanted; whereas the Norman foundations needed land that would support, perhaps, five hundred people: land with a value. How did this come about? The seven thousand fighting men who had proved triumphant at Hastings were rewarded with grants of land and, now being good Catholics, many of them saw it as appropriate to establish a monastery to the Glory of God on a part of their new landholding. (Their ideas of what a monastery should be were, no doubt, strongly influenced by Cluny.) The monks would be expected to say masses for the soul of their Lord, both in this world and in the next. And the possession of a monastery would probably enhance the Lord's political status as well as providing him with a resting place for his dead relatives, and for himself in due course. Adjacent to the monastery he might found a nunnery which could serve as a useful parking place for female relatives who were no longer valuable as pawns in the marriage market. The monastery

THE CHURCH IN NORMAN ENGLAND AND ON INTO THE PLANTAGENETS (1066 to 1399)

built by this Norman lord had to reach certain standards: it had to be a credit to him in the eyes of the neighbours; it also had to be acceptable to the monks who had to live there (passing over their vows of poverty). It was not unknown for a community of monks to up-sticks and move to someone else's monastery, leaving our first Norman lord with an empty building and egg on his face. So standards had to be kept high.

The Celtic Saints had seen their independence and their isolation as an essential feature of their function: as a link and a pathway between God and the human community. The monks of a Norman foundation were different: they were team players; following a rule-book and looking to an authority in Rome. And Rome had memories stretching back to Constantine and to Theodosius. 'Christianity must stick to the one straight path and work in partnership with the State.' (The notes at the end of Chapter Twelve painted a picture of Anglo-Saxon man in the middle of the tenth century, lamenting the passing of 'Celtic Christianity.' So change had already started a century before the Battle of Hastings, but it was the arrival of the Normans that brought down the real hammer blow of change.)

Moving on to the invasion and its aftermath — first thing to say is that not every man who accompanied William the Conqueror had Viking blood firing through his veins. There were Flemish and Breton fighters as well as the get-rich kids who attached themselves to any mediaeval battle. It is also true, of course, that Normans fought on horseback; a new type of warfare and not part of a Viking tradition. However, William and his senior men were claiming to be Christian — they carried a banner presented to them by the Pope — but their thought patterns and intentions were not far distant from the Viking traditions of their recent past. To give ourselves something of a feel for their background, here are a few notes on the world as seen through Viking eyes.

In mediaeval times there were only two descriptions for the creation of the world — the Christian one, and the Norse (or

THE CHURCH IN NORMAN ENGLAND AND ON INTO THE PLANTAGENETS (1066 to 1399)

Viking) one. Some have suggested that the Greek Pantheon should be added to this list of two but, for me, that is a bit too fanciful to find a place here. "And the earth was without form, and void; and darkness was upon the face of the deep." (Genesis 1:2) This serves equally well for either the Christian or the Norse start point. On the Norse path, various gods come on the scene, each doing a bit towards creating a world into which mankind can be introduced. (Not wildly different from the idea of the Garden of Eden.) Gods and Giants are two parts of the Norse world which Christian thinking finds difficult to understand. They were certainly not just 'good' and 'evil', for the Giants were huge, and coarse, and violent, as well as carrying wisdom and knowledge and having creative powers. Friction between Gods and Giants seems to generate the power on which the world runs. Into this newly-formed world come three young women, who are giants. They create man, and fate, and death: and they also create the time within which man is to live. Time starts, and then rolls on with many battles until 'Ragnarok' when, as in any good Viking story, man dissolves into fighting; all is chaos; the world burns and is swallowed by the ocean. All comes to an end, leaving behind a vision of a new world emerging from the ocean where a new generation of gods will rule and mankind will be re-created to live happily ever after.

> "And I saw a new heaven and a new earth; for the first heaven and the first earth were passed away,"
>
> (Revelations 21:1)

Which came first, Norse or Christian? I don't know. Was one derived from the other — now there's a thought!

So William and his army arrived in England in 1066, waving the Pope's banner and proclaiming a Christianity with roots going back to Charlemagne, to Theodosios, and to Constantine: Christianity

THE CHURCH IN NORMAN ENGLAND AND ON INTO THE PLANTAGENETS (1066 to 1399)

with a strong element of civil government embedded within it. And, behind all this, a tradition that saw fighting and battle as a way of working out the purpose of the gods.

Back in Chapter Twelve there was brief mention of the impact Norman thinking had on the English village church, and this chapter has already sketched something of the ideas that led the newly-arrived Normans to build monasteries; it is now time to have a more general look at changes the Normans brought to Christian practices in England. It all starts, I suppose, with the foundation of a Benedictine monastery at Cluny in 909, which became the leader in what I have already called a 'Charlemagne revival'. Cluny (about forty miles north of Lyon) was dedicated to St Paul and St Peter and this might be expected to have given the monastery a close relationship with the Pope but, as we have already seen, the Papacy was in its low period, so Cluny developed on its own, with very little external influence. Cluniac reform laid great stress upon the words of the Bible, and on how these words took precedence over the material wishes of secular rulers. Cluny was also keen to demonstrate the importance and the power of Christian mysteries and rituals, introducing elaborate and magnificent celebrations. This display of wealth attracted more wealth, and donations of land and money flowed in as the Cluniac way of doing things spread across mainland Europe. Curiously, Cluny started to campaign against the excesses of the rich! They also relaunched that familiar Christian campaign against married clergy, only this time the problem was not so much the distractions of sex and a warm bed, more about concern that a married bishop would be moving heaven and earth to ensure that his son would inherit, not only his wealth, but his position in the church. (It is interesting to recall that in far-away Byzantium a very similar line of thought had led to the advancement of eunuchs!) In the eyes of the Church, ever careful to preserve its wealth, any money held by a churchman should return to the Church upon his death.

THE CHURCH IN NORMAN ENGLAND AND ON INTO THE PLANTAGENETS (1066 to 1399)

After the invasion, as England came under Norman control, subtle changes started to affect the Church. As an incumbent died, or retired, or was ejected, his place was awarded to a Frenchman or an Italian with good Cluniac background. These newcomers seem to have been chosen for their organisational skills rather than for any spiritual devotion of the sort we might imagine filled the souls of Anglo-Saxon monks. Something of an 'old pals network' was being built up with Lanfranc at the centre. Lanfranc had been born in Italy, he became a monk at the Abbey of Bec in Normandy and a spiritual advisor to William, soon to become the Conqueror: he taught the man who went on to become Pope Alexander II (the Pope who gave his blessing to William's invasion plans). Lanfranc was made Archbishop of Canterbury in 1070 and did duty as Regent when William was away following his continental interests. William and Lanfranc working together made an amazing change to England. Within the space of one lifetime: a new aristocracy, a new language, changes to social structure and laws, as well as changes to churches and, one might almost say, changes in attitude towards Christianity itself. Church and State should henceforth run along together as one well-oiled machine, or so the plan suggested. Constantine must have looked down from above with approval. Google offers a relevant quote from the Catholic Encyclopaedia, 1913: - "The insularity of the native clergy was thus beneficially broken down"!

As part of the eleventh century Reformation (if that is the right word) some centres for Bishoprics were moved, perhaps to get bishops away from strong centres of traditional Anglo-Saxon belief. Again the Catholic Encyclopaedia has a quote: -

> "Many episcopal sees were at this period (1070's) transferred from obscure villages to rising towns, as Sherbourne to Salisbury, Dorchester (Oxon) to Lincoln, Thetford to Norwich and Selsey to Chichester."

THE CHURCH IN NORMAN ENGLAND AND ON INTO THE PLANTAGENETS (1066 to 1399)

In the early years after 1066, there was still a small number of slaves being transferred to new owners as ownership of the land was revised, and the slave trade between Bristol and Dublin was still in business, but the Normans had a different approach to these matters. To a Norman lord, all the people on his land were, to some extent, his people; they had obligations to him and, to a lesser extent, he had obligations to them. With such a system, there was no longer an advantage in owning slaves. Indeed, a Norman villein could be regarded as a slave, but without the food and shelter that a slave-owner would normally provide: he had to find his own. Then if a Norman lord built a church, there can be little doubt all his villeins would attend! A full church would clearly demonstrate that the Norman way of doing things was the right way to go.

Ideas of marriage also underwent a change. Before Norman times a man and a woman could simply agree to become married. It was, after all, a civil contract sealed by intercourse. It may have been a good idea to let your friends know, but I don't think it was essential. Certainly the Church was not involved in any way. After the Normans had become established, Cluniac Christianity saw itself as responsible for guiding human life in all its aspects, and took over the concept of marriage. To be valid, marriage was now to be celebrated in church or at least in the church porch, with vows made before God. (I think there was a pre-meeting in the church porch to settle matters of money and land, before going into the church for the wedding.) And before long, the Church began to have a say in who could marry whom, starting off from the sensible idea that two people who were close blood relations should not marry each other, and going on to a ban on marriages between cousins up to the seventh degree (whatever that means). Then a ban on marriage to the children of godparents, who were of course your spiritual relatives. Think of a rustic couple living in the same village: some clash in their bloodlines was almost inevitable if you looked hard enough. Moving into the world of the rich and noble, the selection of a marriage partner was governed by the

THE CHURCH IN NORMAN ENGLAND AND ON INTO THE PLANTAGENETS (1066 to 1399)

requirements of inheritance, leading to a restricted choice, with close relationships difficult to avoid. Again, with the Church holding records of marriage, it was the Church that could identify the true heir to the family wealth and dismiss the bastard claimants. Add to this the rule that you must not marry your brother's widow and we begin to see that the Church had granted itself powers to intervene in very many proposed marriages. Some of these awkwardness's could of course be overcome by a suitable donation.

With this formalisation of marriage came the idea that a wife was a possession of her husband; she had no rights or possessions of her own. Any land or wealth she might have had, transferred to her husband upon marriage. (With all my worldly goods I thee endow!) Thus the Church, and to some extent all of male society, saw women as loose cannons — they needed control and direction from a responsible male, either by father, or by husband. With this sort of thinking, a widow was a dangerous wild thing to be captured by another marriage, or lodged in a nunnery as soon as possible. It is not entirely clear whether this picture of male dominance over women came down through the Norman line, from a history of Viking rape and pillage, or whether it was a result of Christian teaching. All the teachers of Christianity (except one) had had a bit of a problem with women. Apart from the one woman who came into this world without original sin, all the rest were daughters of Eve and could easily become a trap and a distraction for right-thinking men. There was however one small light in all this social engineering. Legal punishments were either capital, or a fine of money (imprisonment was not an available punishment in a mediaeval court). Thus a married woman, provided she kept away from treason and murder, could do whatever she liked without fear of the law because she had neither land nor money and so could not be fined. This legal loophole must have added to a man's uncertainty about women.

No longer could a woman go off on pilgrimage without her husband — but then, in 1095, with the announcement of the first crusade, a noblewoman might suddenly find herself with enormous responsibilities, having to run both house and estate as her husband 'took the Cross'.

This change from the Christianity of Lindisfarne to the Christianity of Cluny is well illustrated by Trevor Rowley in his book 'The Normans'. He writes: "Lanfranc's kinsman, Abbot Paul, broke the tombs of the former abbots of St Albans whom he referred to as 'uncultured idiots'." Rowley goes on to quote William of Malmesbury, writing about 1125, "England has become a residence for foreigners and the property of aliens. At the present time there is no English earl, nor bishop, nor abbot; strangers all, they prey upon the riches and vitals of England," The Battle of Hastings begins to look like only one small part in the takeover of England.

*****

That mention of the first crusade, happening only one generation after William's conquest, is another marker for a change in Christian thinking. Back in the years just before 1000 there had been a fear in the air that the world would come to an end with the millennium (Armageddon or Ragnarok according to taste). The rising power of Viking forces provided some reason to give support to this fear — but it didn't happen! That same fear came alive again in the run-up to 1100 and it may have been a component thought within the Pope's plan for a Christian army to drive the Muslims out of Jerusalem in time for the Second Coming in 1100.

There have been many books about the Crusades, and I have no wish to add to their number, but Crusader thinking had an effect on life in England and here I do have an interest.

Pope Urban II was the son of a noble family and had spent time as a monk at Cluny. Urban was keen to re-establish connections between the Christian communities of Byzantium and Rome, but there was a centralising authority growing in the Curia and in the College of Cardinals that barred his progress in that direction, so I think his mind turned to Jerusalem. I think that we might assume, when Urban made his famous speech at Clermont in 1095, the ideas in his mind were something like this.

Mainland Europe was a very unsettled place at the time, with much minor conflict going on, with younger sons of the aristocracy and robber barons trying to improve their lot by stealing off the neighbours or taking their land. Would it not be a grand idea if all these aggressive young men could be gathered together to fight for the 'One Worth-while Project' and head east, leaving Europe quiet? Unfortunately, what happened was slightly different. Something of a child-like obedience heard the Pope's call for crusade. Down tools and go to liberate Jerusalem: God will provide! What the Pope had expected were groups of men with some experience of fighting, under some sort of leader — what he got was large numbers of men straight from the fields, with no experience and no recognised leaders, all setting off for Jerusalem on foot. God did indeed provide! The Crusaders took their food from the fields and storehouses of the lands they walked through. History offers no record of the thousands of deaths from starvation in the lands stripped bare of food by passing Crusaders. Jewish communities suffered particularly badly: many Christians saw the Jews as the people who had killed Jesus, and so, many Jews were killed and their money and goods reallocated to help the Crusade. God was indeed providing!

The Norman invasion of England had, as it were, added a new department to Christian thinking: a department concerned with social management and control. 'Crusader thinking' was also to make an addition: so long as you waved your banner and followed the Cross, then if people along the way got robbed or killed, this was little matter: it all fell into place beside the wider Christian objectives! This entry of a certain brutality into Christian thinking may have been the start that led onward, in later years, to Christians being burnt at the stake for failing to believe in the transubstantiation of the bread and wine. The Muslims found all this very difficult to understand: indeed, Muslim records of the time are very few and show nothing of the triumphalist outcry of Christian writings.

(As a footnote: - it was not until the late eighteenth century that the world of Islam saw the rise of strongly militaristic groups. Groups that laid particular emphasis on selected verses from the Koran and were quite prepared to fight and die for their beliefs. Like the Christian Crusaders, they were assured that death in battle would result in an immediate transfer to Paradise. Early groups of this sort were associated with the name 'Wahhabi' and, moving on into more recent times, 'Mujahedeen', 'Al-Qaeda' and 'Islamic State'. For these groups, 'Jehad' became a battle cry against everyone they saw as non-believers, and the cry had lost the subtlety of its earlier sense of a 'struggle to protect the wider Muslim community'!) This vision of a paradise in the next world has done much to create misery in this.

The eleven hundreds and the twelve hundreds saw the people of England coming to terms with a new approach to Christianity. No more the quiet and reflective ways of the old pre-Viking monasteries and churches. New ideas of show and ceremony with beginnings at Cluny two hundred years ago, started to trickle into England with Saint Dunstan, but it was under the new Norman lords that we got the full treatment. A new Norman church in every village teaching the Christian message in the language of Rome, and taking over authority for village management. As suggested above, Crusader activities had taught Christians that the single-minded pursuit of their faith left a few dead and damaged bodies along the wayside. Dead and damaged bodies began to appear, painted onto church walls as a threat to all who might fail to come up to expected church standards! Scenes from the torture chambers of hell reminded churchgoers of what would await them if they strayed from the path of Church teaching. These pictures were no doubt intended to operate at a personal level. (This is what might happen if you do not mend your ways!) but the pictures got wider, and we saw DOOM! Pictures of Christ himself presiding over the separation of good people destined for heaven; from the bad people destined for hell. (Roughly equal numbers in the pictures I have seen!) Religious thinking had moved on from "love your neighbour", to "do what I tell you or else —!" It may have been the harshness of this situation that led to the invention of Purgatory.

It should not escape twenty-first century thinking that this whole topic turned around the expectation of what was to happen after death. The Church claimed to know, and there was no evidence to contradict. No one had come back! The Church persuaded the people that if they did not follow Church rules — it would be nasty! Thus the Church had a strong lever with which to control people. My sketchy knowledge of all the major world religions suggests that they all follow a very similar path: as ye sow in this world, so shall ye reap in the next! Perhaps they are right?

I don't think there are many people around today who look forward to a bodily resurrection, so for most of us it is into the ground, or up in smoke: in either case, the particulates returning to the physical world from which they came. So what of mind, and what of soul? Of mind, one can say that Socrates is still alive, for his work is studied to this day. At a more ordinary level, we all live on by what we have built or by the children we have raised. Soul is a much more difficult concept. It has to do with 'faith' and 'belief', both words that lack a solid and comforting anchor into 'our' world. "I believe" is a statement that no-one can contradict, for it has this upward link. Faith and belief both point to a higher world, a world in which earth-bound words are of little use: a land Socrates called the World of Form; a land we could usefully think of as a world of soul. In extreme distress we might send out an SOS. (Save our Souls — the most important part of us.) As an aside, we might see a reason behind Theodosius's attempt to destroy memory of the Greek

THE CHURCH IN NORMAN ENGLAND AND ON INTO THE PLANTAGENETS (1066 to 1399)

philosophers, and transfer their idea of 'soul' and all that went with it, into the Christian world.

So the picture of England under William I shows a largely agricultural land where the majority work at food production, some to be eaten, some to be stored, some to be sold for money, some to be delivered to their lord by way of rent, some to go onward to the King, and some to go to the church or monastery as a religious due. So long as the demands were reasonable, the system worked. But kings decide to go to war; or a lord wants to heighten the walls of his castle, or an abbot wants more silver vessels for the altar, and a gold cross —.

Life in a monastery was hard: indeed, it was designed to be so. Then ideas from the French monastery at Cluny introduced formal ceremony and display into church services, and as income increased, the display got grander. So the monks following this Benedictine Order grew accustomed to seeing wealth on display. Although monks had, of course, taken a vow of poverty, they saw no conflict in living in grand buildings and handling things of great monetary value. (All to the Glory of God!) Bring this thought pattern into Norman England, where the Norman ancestors, the Vikings, were noted for their lust after gold and silver — and a pattern begins to form in the mind. (Visions of wealth, and with it, comfort.)

(It might also bring into mind the present day situation where a television screen has shown 'Western Wealth' to an ever-increasing population of the world's poor — result, a mass migration towards the honey-pot. What had taken three, four, five generations to build up, is wanted NOW!)

The later eleventh century and into the twelfth saw monasteries caught up in this infection of wealth that was in the air. Their prayer routines became less rigorous and much of their physical labour was passed on to the lay brothers who began to look much more like a paid labour force. And the food got better! There was of course a

THE CHURCH IN NORMAN ENGLAND AND ON INTO THE PLANTAGENETS (1066 to 1399)

reaction: there was discontent at the state of the monasteries. New monasteries came to be built and a new order of monks founded with the object of going back to proper religious observance and discipline. This turned out to be a repeating process: the slide down into easy living, followed by the foundation of a new order with smartly pulled-up socks.

A new start had been made in the tenth century using the ideas of Christianity that came out of the attempt by Charlemagne and Pope Leo to reconstruct the Roman Empire back in the 800's. Ideas that had been taken up with enthusiasm by the Abbey at Cluny. In England, St. Dunstan worked with these ideas coming over from France and started to construct a new monastic world, but it was not until the arrival of the Normans with lots and lots of money that things really began to move. (Back in Chapter Ten I drew attention to a link between Vikings, Money and Christianity. The Vikings may have changed their name to 'Normans', but — Here We Are Again!)

The central feature of this Rome-flavoured monasticism was the 'Rule of Saint Benedict', set down in the middle of the sixth century and incorporated into Charlemagne's world in 816. This 'Rule' was the basis for what was seen as proper monastic life. The service of 'Matins' started the monastic day at 2am, but what this actually meant, in the years before clocks, is very unclear. (As a footnote, the very first mechanical clocks were invented around the fourteenth century for this very purpose: marking the hours within a religious community.)

From the days of Dunstan and before, there seem to have been some religious houses that followed the teachings of St. Augustine (of Hippo). They seem to have moved among the lay community in much the same way as the Friars were to do some three hundred years later. (Was this perhaps a pattern left over from the days before the Viking Destruction?) Men following this looser way of religious life tended to be called canons, rather than monks.

THE CHURCH IN NORMAN ENGLAND AND ON INTO THE PLANTAGENETS (1066 to 1399)

The monks of the tenth century were referred to as 'Benedictines' because of the Rule they followed, while some came to be called Clunaics or Cluniacs after their parent monastery at Cluny. (They were the ones noted for good food!) Then, as Norman wealth was put into building monasteries, we saw the arrival of Carthusians, Augustinians, Cistercians and Premonstratensians, all within the short period from 1084 to 1120 or thereabouts, and each claiming to follow the 'Rule' more closely than their predecessors. Some of the building techniques are of interest to an ex-engineer. Build during the summer period only: leaving the winter months for settlement to take place. Then in the next building season, carry on, but do your best to correct any out-of-line, or out-of-plumb caused by last winter's settlement. High towers were very popular: but if your two-hundred-foot tower fell down — replace it with a hundred and fifty-foot tower! ('Model analysis' at a one to one scale!) Part of these building costs were met by the monks and nuns themselves, for in order to enter a monastery or nunnery, you would be expected to bring with you a sizeable donation of money or land. In some cases, the size of your donation had an effect on your subsequent lifestyle. Silvia Evangelisti, in her book 'Nuns', tells of two classes, Choir Nuns and Servant Nuns: the servant nuns, in addition to their religious duties, were required to act as servants to the choir nuns. Servant nuns were not permitted education or the pursuit of literacy for fear it would impede their servant function. Not surprisingly there are very few surviving records of this sort of arrangement within enclosed houses of monks or nuns.

There seems to have been a general pattern throughout the monastic period in England of a slow decline in discipline, followed by a sharp intake of breath and a return to something more like the Rule of Saint Benedict. In an attempt to reduce distraction, the Cistercian monks built their monasteries in remote locations, Fountains Abbey of 1130 being a well-known example. Another characteristic of the Cistercians was that they would only accept donations to their Order in the form of land. Thus all monasteries,

THE CHURCH IN NORMAN ENGLAND AND ON INTO THE PLANTAGENETS (1066 to 1399)

and the Cistercians in particular, accumulated huge tracts of land. Now twelfth and thirteenth century England saw the rising success of the wool trade and a clear way to financial profit was in the raising of sheep. Thus monasteries became sheep farmers on a grand scale. On monastic land there had once been villages, each with its fields on which the villagers grew their food. In the monasteries New Look, sheep farming did not require labour — so out with the villagers and their patches of agricultural land — and in with more sheep. A similar process took place six hundred years later in Scotland, where landlords expelled tenants in order to make way for more sheep, the so-called 'Highland Clearances' — but the monks got their first! Repeat after me, "Normans, Money, then Christianity!"

(In fairness to the story of the Highland Clearances, I should perhaps point out that the climate of England and Scotland in the seventeenth and eighteenth centuries went into a marked decline and the poor people scraping a bare living on the Scottish hills could no longer feed themselves. Landowners saw a solution in encouraging the people to emigrate — with varying degrees of force.)

The early thirteenth century saw the arrival in England of the Friars — Franciscans, Dominicans, Carmelites and Austin Friars. Friars saw their religious duty as teaching and preaching to the lay community and were thus a much more visible force than the more or less enclosed orders of monks and nuns. And, as Friars worked with people, they chose to live in or near towns. Way back in Chapter Two I made some fairly light-hearted comments about the interrelation between monks, friars and the newly developing Oxford University. It is now time to try and fit those thoughts into a general flow of history.

THE CHURCH IN NORMAN ENGLAND AND ON INTO THE PLANTAGENETS (1066 to 1399)

Fountains Abbey – North Yorkshire (1130)

The very first signs of teaching at Oxford had been noted in 1096, with some expansion of student numbers recorded in 1167, but it was around 1250 that these newly arrived friars, and some monks, moved into Oxford and began to play a part in the University's development. One can imagine two alternative lines of thought at this point.

1. This new development of intellectual thought needs to be guided into the path of right thinking that had been established within the Roman Church since the days of Constantine.

2. Or, more than eight hundred years ago Theodosius had determined that Nicaean Christianity was the only path to be followed, and that all other knowledge was to be discarded. Could it be that this gathering together of ideas, called a 'University', might mark a re-awakening of ideas that Theodosius thought he had killed off? Alarm bells started to ring in the Papal Office.

THE CHURCH IN NORMAN ENGLAND AND ON INTO THE PLANTAGENETS (1066 to 1399)

Thought number 1 was not a problem; the Church was well accustomed to giving guidance along a well-trodden path. Thought 2 was a much more dangerous idea. It allowed freedom of thought, and who knows where that might lead? It could (and eventually did) break up the monopoly of the Roman Church. It may have been chance; it may have been a deliberate Papal plan; or it may have been an Act of God — but a solution was found — and Thought number 1 won! (At least for the next three hundred years or so.)

Men of the Holy Orders, Friars and Monks, had taken a vow of obedience, so when they were told to join a University — they went. Money was no problem for their parent House paid all their costs and expenses without question. (I have to admit, at this point, that I have no knowledge of the numbers, or the proportion, of Friars, Monks or other clerics, compared with non-clerical students at Oxford, or any other University. As suggested in Chapter Two, one might expect clerical students — who were paid for — to outnumber lay students who had to pay their own bills.) If we now remember the old trading axiom, "The customer is always right", and also remembering where much of university funding was coming from, we begin to see a reason why religion grew to become a dominant part of university education, with 'Theology' top of the pile and 'canon law' not far behind. You could, of course, argue that in a world without the technology, the science, and the arts that fill our present day universities, in a simpler world of the thirteenth century, theology would rise naturally to the top of any list of studies. Perhaps.

Things chugged along for the next hundred years or so, then Western Europe was hit by a big bang! Bubonic plague, or the Black Death. There are of course no statistics for the middle of the fourteenth century: I was brought up with the rule of three: one third escaped infection: one third caught it and recovered: one third caught it and died. Modern thinking seems to favour something more like a 50% death toll, and no doubt it varied from place to place. Anyway, food production was heavily labour intensive so a loss of manpower, be it 33% or 50%, was a critical matter for it disrupted all the existing systems and hunger threatened. Before this Black Death of 1349, our history books usually give an impression of the working man, the peasant, labouring in the fields without complaint. A state of man ordained by God! (One needs to ask yet again, who wrote the history?) Standard thinking suggests that a drop in the labour force would put up the value of the labourer, and we see a 'Peasant's Revolt' in 1381. A dangerous uprising, defused by a royal promise that was withdrawn as soon as the forces of 'law and order' had regained control.

Running in parallel with this shake-up in English society, there was a shake-up within the Papacy. In 1378, Pope Urban VI was elected. He had a background as a canon lawyer and as an archbishop but, rather more to the point, he was born in Naples which makes him securely Italian; always an important factor in Papal elections. All seemed well until the Pope went mad! I am sorry to use brutal language: the official line seems to be 'he had an unstable temperament'. A second Pope was elected, Clement VII 'The First'. (Not to be confused with Pope Clement VII 'The Second' who appears in the essay on Henry VIII.) Pope Urban refused to stand down, so there were two Popes, Urban and Clement, each excommunicating the other. There followed a period of thirty-nine years, called 'the Great Schism' when there were two, and sometimes three Popes, many of whom spent their time struggling to get their hands on as much money as they could.

This period at the very end of the fourteenth century saw England's first popular book — 'The Canterbury Tales' by Geoffrey Chaucer. Chaucer had held several important government posts and so we can see him as a respected member of society, but his Tales included fun from the disreputable end of the church structure: men who claimed authority to forgive sins — for a suitable payment, and men who would sell you an 'absolutely genuine' fragment of a saint. Thus humour seems to have become

THE CHURCH IN NORMAN ENGLAND AND ON INTO THE PLANTAGENETS (1066 to 1399)

acceptable at the bottom end of Church activity — at least, nobody tried to burn Chaucer — but beware! For serious thinkers there was still danger! Over on the Continent, in 1415, Jan Hus was burnt at the stake; his bones gathered up from the ashes, so that they could be broken into small pieces and thrown into the river. (All to avoid a martyrs burial site.) His crime? A suggestion that the Church would do well to model itself on life as portrayed in the Bible, and not concentrate its efforts on the gathering of wealth. First the Vikings; then their children, the Normans; and now the Roman Church — each in their turn pursuing wealth. And, one might almost add, 'without regard for human life!' The devil must have been clapping his hands!

CHAPTER FOURTEEN
MONEY AND REFORMATION

Almost every English village has a church. And most village churches have an origin that goes back to the three hundred years that followed the Norman invasion. What did they cost? Few of us have any grasp on the value of William's silver pennies, so let us think in terms of present day money. Appeals for a new roof, or other substantial repairs, commonly run into five or six figures. So what is a modern figure for building the whole church from scratch? It has to be a couple of million. Labour costs would have been lower in the past, but then the transport of materials would have been far more expensive. So, one or two million pounds to build a church to serve a population of, perhaps, one hundred households. Then, of course, a few generations on there would be the start of mutterings. 'Our church is old fashioned'. Can we get away with a bit of re-styling; or is it a full re-build? Another million or two into the pot. Something else to consider is that half a day's walk away, there would be a market town and this would probably have a monastery (say twenty million for building that). Oh yes, I nearly forgot, there was a nunnery as well — anther twenty million!

Many will say that this is all nonsense — and I'm inclined to agree with you. My purpose has been to illustrate the dominance of the Church over the economics of the time. There was no local authority; no health service; you had to look after yourself: a bit of a struggle to buy cloth to make clothes for the kids. But out there — somewhere out of sight — huge sums were moving around and the Church seemed to be doing very well. Norman method had loosened up the money supply and you can't, after all, build a cheap church: it has to be done to the Glory of God! (Once again that familiar link — Normans, Money, Christianity.)

History seems to suggest that this pattern of village life went on with little change until the major disruption of 1349; Black Death! Economics tell us that a reduction in the labour force should lead to a rise in wages, but the gentry of the time fought to resist any such change. Perhaps out of this tension arose a general feeling of unrest.

Too much of the wealth generated by sweat in field and village was being fossilised as elegant stonework. Time to move on.

I have done a little work on local churches and formed an impression (I leave it to others to do the proper fieldwork). The history of my idealised English Village Church looks something like this.

The Church of All Saints, somewhere in the southern half of England

Tradition tells us that the first church on this site was built by the Normans in the eleventh century, although there are only a few stones re-positioned in the tower from that date. There is some evidence for twelfth century work in the nave but the chancel was rebuilt in the thirteenth and a tower added in the fourteenth. Then a coat of whitewash under the Puritans, followed by seats (!) and extensive redecoration by the Victorians. Currently the plan is to take out the fixed seating to allow space for other activities.

(Which can be interpreted as, 'Not much by way of major building works after the Black Death'.)

So, as the fourteenth century drew to a close, with social unrest following in the wake of the Black Death, and with an uncomfortable feeling in the air that the plague had been a punishment sent from God for something we had done wrong: and with a sense of change as the Royal House of Plantagenet (the successors to the Normans) faded away; we saw less money being spent on the extension and rebuilding of churches. After three hundred years that stable triangle of 'Normans, Money,

Christianity' had crumbled. The Normans had gone: the money had — what had happened to the money? Remember we are still in the middle of The Great Schism (1378 to 1417), a time of multiple Popes, most of whom worked hard to draw into Papal funds as much money as possible and there were three Papal Cities to support, Rome, Avignon and Pisa. (A situation that has already had mention in the essay on Henry VIII.) The 'Sale of Indulgences' had been around since the announcement of the First Crusade in 1095. (By a suitable payment to the Church, or to a Church Officer, you could reduce the length of your expected stay in Purgatory, and speed up your transfer to Heaven — or so everybody had been taught to believe.) I have little doubt that in the time of the Great Schism, the gathering of money from the sale of indulgencies approached 'industrial' scale. And with the return of the Papacy to a more normal basis in 1417, I see no sign of a return to the earlier, more moderate level. There was clearly an uneasiness growing within the Church, but it must have been difficult to argue for a reduction of income, particularly when we were rebuilding St Peter's in Rome. Proposals for reform were pushed to one side until the Council of Trent finally opened in 1545. But the train had already departed! Martin Luther had nailed his thesis to the church door in 1517: King Henry had separated England from Rome in 1534 and Calvin had set up in Geneva in 1541. How much are we talking about Christianity, and how much are we talking about money? Your choice!

*****

REFORMATION (My dictionary says, 'Radical change for the better!')

In continental Europe 'Reformation' focuses on Martin Luther (1483 – 1546) and his protest that the Church of Rome had become corrupted by an excessive interest in money. Those who shared similar views came to be called 'Protestants'. There is little doubt that there were many in England who thought along the same lines, and had concern for the way that Church and Monastery had acquired major influence on the money flow in their country. BUT: in England, attention was focussed on King Henry, and on his problem in begetting a legitimate male heir. Generations of historians have found this latter story more interesting.

Thus, from the ideas first seen in John Wycliff and Jan Hus back in the fourteenth century, there had grown a movement that was substantial enough to stand up against Catholic Rome. As Catholic squared up against Protestant, it is my suspicion that the History of Christianity underwent, what shall we say, 'a simplification'.

> Had not Jesus Christ himself given instructions to Peter and to Paul about the proper foundation of His Church? And had not the two of them travelled to Rome for this very purpose? Peter had initiated the office of Pope, and Christ's authority, descending in the person of the Pope, had come down in an unbroken chain to us in the present day.

I feel that a present day Roman Catholic would be reasonably happy to go along with this as a pocket history. But anyone who has paid attention to this book will be aware that there is other material to be considered.

Let us consider the letter 'S'. Not one Reformation, but many Reformations.

Reformation 1 In the earliest days, Christians can be seen as a quiet semi-secret group living under an alien authority. As time went by, 'bishops' appeared who took up a position of authority over the 'ordinary' Christians. Some bishops were personally ambitious and some were experimenting with variations in belief. Antony retreated into the desert around 285 looking for a quieter life.

Reformation 2 The first Ecumenical Council at Nicaea in 325. (Pause for a moment and think of the date, two hundred and ninety-five years after the death of Christ, then ask yourself how well you understand England in the reign of King George I? And we have history books!) Constantine was rebuilding the Roman Empire — his Empire — centred on Constantinople — in a world of Greek language and tradition. It seems probable that Constantine and his agents reviewed the various Christian ideas that were circulating among the Greek speakers, and made a selection that would fit in well with his re-constructed empire.

Reformation 3 The Second Ecumenical Council at Constantinople in 381. The soldier, now Emperor, Theodosius lays down the law. Unswerving attachment to Nicaean thinking is now required and this led to the 'heresy hunting' and the destruction of any material that pre-dated Nicaea. (The Dawn of the Dark Ages.) In 385 a bishop was beheaded for thinking differently.

Reformation 4 Christianity begins to spread with the desert traders of the East. Metropolitans (Archbishops) established as far away as Beijing. Great activity in Egypt and Syria developing Monastic ideas of Christian life (and seeds from Egypt seem to find their way to Britain).

Reformation 5 The Fourth Ecumenical Council at Chalcedon in 451. Following a technical difference of theology, Rome takes Western Europe along a different path from that taken by Africa and Asia. What had looked like the Grand Expansion of Christianity, misfires. Christianity lives on in Iran, China, Mongolia, Egypt and Ethiopia, but the Christians of Europe do not see it.

Reformation 6 A mysterious happening, for which history offers no evidence. The centre of Christian authority and power moves from the Greek world to Rome. And changes language from Greek (so well-suited to detailed theological debate) to Latin (so well-suited to issuing commands and instructions). From the time of St Peter, the Pope had been based in Rome, following on, perhaps, from Imperial times and Rome's obvious geographical advantages. So, I am sure, a Good Catholic would see Christianity as 'coming home.'

Reformation 7 Pope Gregory the Great (590 – 604) did much to tidy up the Christianity of Western Europe, but he did not get on well with the Church in Constantinople. Christianity is fast becoming the religion of Western Europe, centred on Rome, with Christians in other parts of the world dropping off the membership list. The dramatic expansion of the Muslim faith in the 660's and the 670's saw the Middle East, Egypt and the North African coast move out of the reach of Christian influence. (My cynical self adds "Thus simplifying the situation!)

Reformation 8 We have already looked at the scheme hatched up by Pope Leo III and the Emperor Charlemagne, culminating with the creation of 'The Holy Roman Empire' on Christmas Day 800. Once again we see Christianity being 'adjusted' to serve as a tool for civil government.

*****

Enough of the numbering sequence: we go on to see Charlemagne's system collapse under disagreement among his children, only to be revived a century later as part of the reconstruction after Viking devastation. As Vikings change into Normans and take up Christianity, something of the Power of the Viking re-surfaces as a Power of the Christian Church. (Look at the speed and number of church constructions in England.) Power eventually slides into greed, then indulgences lead us back to Martin Luther!

It is easy to complain at this point that our story is heavy on the politics of government, whilst the emotional side of spiritual belief is barely visible. One might argue, I suppose, that it is the fire of emotion that pushes the politics around. On the other hand, an experienced politician can see public emotion as something to be manipulated. It brings us back to the title of this book, "History and Religion — An Uncomfortable Relationship".

To study how people, behave, is politics. To study how people ought to behave begins to look like religion.

CHAPTER FIFTEEN
SOME LEFT-OVER THOUGHTS

From hints already scattered in this book, it is clear that Vikings have had a far greater effect upon our history than is usually admitted. In the year 800, Charlemagne and Pope Leo started work to establish a powerful Christian Church solidly based in Rome: while, at a very similar time, but in far-away Norway, men were inventing sea-going warships and becoming Vikings. The one part going on to assemble wealth: the other part seeking wealth.

At a vague date, somewhere around the year 1000, the Viking world seems to have taken up Christianity. But I don't think this meant quite what Rome hoped it meant. In fact, I don't think it meant very much at all. Back in Chapter Thirteen there was a quick sketch of Viking religious beliefs and I suggest that for your average Viking in the street there was no difference worth bothering about. But being a Christian did give you a voice at the 'top table', and Christianity worn as a lapel badge could be taken off whenever there was an advantage to be gained. Blend Viking strength and aggression with Roman self-assurance and you set the pattern for English history, from the Battle of Hastings to the Battle of Bosworth (1066-1485). Four hundred years largely filled with mediaeval warfare. Here was the nightmare that later flared in Henry VIII's mind; unless he could provide a legitimate male heir, his sixteenth century world would slide back into this mediaeval mayhem, where kings wanted money to raise armies and Roman churches wanted money to increase their own grandeur. The old three elements: - Vikings turned Norman; Christianity turned Roman; and the universal lubricant, money.

> (We should not, perhaps, be too harsh on these four hundred years of mediaeval English history. They did, after all, suggest the plots for most of Shakespeare's historical plays and they saw the building of castles and cathedrals that provide highlights for any holiday tour of this country. And

not to mention the church that forms the centre-piece in a thousand English villages.)

*****

King Henry VIII's parents-in-law highlight a very different story, but one that reveals a familiar theme. Ferdinand and Isabella gave authority and funds to support adventurers sailing westward out across the Atlantic Ocean with a three-fold objective: to get control of the best trade routes; to bring new lands into the sweep of the Spanish Empire, and to gather up the souls of poor benighted savages into the comfort of the Roman Catholic religion. But very soon, all these ideas were swept aside by the hunt for GOLD! I once visited the Sanctuary of Ignatius of Loyola in Northern Spain, home to the Jesuits (The Society of Jesus, founded in 1541). One thing sticks in my mind: a whole wall of gold, into which was set gold-fronted cupboards each holding, we were told, religious relics.

*****

Is it religion that causes wars? As a broad generality we might say that war arises from the usual (male) ambitions for more land, for more wealth and for more control: unless, of course, you are on the other side, in which case it is 'defence'. But religion does provide a focus, the enthusiasm, the energy and something to wave — the chi-rho, at Milvian Bridge; the Papal banner at Hastings, or the black flag for a new Islamic State in Iraq. Religions, that were intended to draw people together, were sprouting barriers. Could it be that human beings are not capable of living as One Big Happy Family? To maintain their energy levels, perhaps they need something or someone to fight for, with, or against. Theoretical Theology versus human nature! Enough of the cynicism — let us move on.

SOME LEFT-OVER THOUGHTS

*****

For a great many people, religion has provided a structure for life. In return for a bit of faith, the Church has an answer for every question. But I have a feeling that things are changing. Numbers in church on an ordinary Sunday morning have declined and there are now many who take care to avoid any activity that carries a whiff of 'church'. On the other hand, since the war, our houses have filled with refrigerators and driers, telephones and television, with a computer in every child's bedroom. Could these changes be related? Once the Church gave us answers: now it is Google. Try entering "Life after Death" into Google and it will offer twenty-five million responses; my Church Service Book reads, "We look for the resurrection of the dead and the life of the world to come." Good comforting lines with a lot of hope, but no awkward detail. A quick flip through World Eschatology (Greek for what happens to us at the end) shows an almost unanimous agreement on the idea that whatever seeds you sow in the world, you will reap in the next. Buddhists and Hindus extend the process by introducing reincarnation but, give or take a rebirth or two, the doctrine of 'As ye sow so shall ye reap' is near universal. Indeed, if you were setting up a new religion of your own, wouldn't you make use of the same idea to keep your flock in order? No one will come back to contradict you.

This, 'As ye sow' line tells us quite a lot about churches, but not very much about the after death experience. Trying not to be ghoulish about a ghoulish subject, a few years underground, or a short stay in a hot box, mark an end to 'us' in any physical sense, although we may leave a trace in the memory of our friends, and a bone or two may land up in an archaeologist's tray. To go further is difficult. None of us like the idea of life coming to a dead stop — and there stands the Church offering us heaven! For anyone with a serious interest, I recommend going back to the days before

SOME LEFT-OVER THOUGHTS

Christianity, to the world of the Greek philosophers, a world the Christians of Constantinople were keen to abandon. 'In the beginning was the Word.' Re-read the last two paragraphs of Chapter Three, for the Greek philosophers probably got as close to this subject as words can get.

*****

Years ago I recall seeing booklets from the Jehovah's Witnesses which showed pictures of the 'next world' looking very like idyllic scenes from a children's story book. Nothing wrong with that, if you feel the need for a picture. Certainly a lot better than views from the torture chambers of hell that some mediaeval churches chose to paint on their walls! If you still feel the need for a picture of life in this world and the next, try this one: -

> Imagine a limitless sea: the wind blows and starts waves here and there: the wind moves on and the waves die down. The sea represents the material world: the waves are life — you, me, and the other six billion. And, of course, the wind is God. Traditional views of heaven and of hell are nowhere to be found, but remember the words of Jesus, "The Father's Kingdom is spread out upon the earth, and people do not see it." (Gospel of Thomas, saying 113)

*****

Can we remind ourselves again how little we know about Christianity in its early formative years: from the days of fishing and shepherding, to the time of Constantine's empire building. Say two hundred and fifty years between a Christianity taught by wandering teachers in a sparsely populated countryside: to

SOME LEFT-OVER THOUGHTS

Christianity as a component in the management of one of the world's largest cities. Some clearly fled into the desert to escape the increasing politics of Christianity. Do we see here the roots of the difference between the Christianity of Lindisfarne, and the Christianity of Cluny?

Indeed, something of these two parts are still with us today. There is the 'Church of Organisation'; the one that makes a splendid job of staging coronations: the one that pays your vicar, and also offers a chain of command down to your local Parochial Church Council where you can go and complain if church bells keep you awake on Sunday morning. And then there is the part that you may only find if you go looking: a modern parallel to the pre-Viking Anglo-Saxon who turned up at the door of a monastery with a question.

*****

By way of revision, let us take another quick flip through Christian history. (As with all this book — a personal view!)

> Start with a new teaching in the thinly populated lands around the Sea of Galilee.
>
> Romans and Jewish leaders see the teaching as a disturbance in the smooth running of their territory.
>
> Paul writes to Christian communities in other locations. (So there had been some spreading out.)
>
> Peter and Paul are thought to live in Rome for around twenty years, but there is little record of their activities. (Presumably because they were living undercover in an antagonistic society.)
>
> Christian ideas spread in lands at the eastern end of the Mediterranean, and in what we now call Greece, Turkey and Egypt.

With this spread and the increasing distances, come different styles of leadership. Some leaders place emphasis on different elements of the teaching. Arius, for example, emphasised the simple style of life as portrayed in the New Testament, while others saw leadership of a Christian group as a way to build up their own personal influence. As already mentioned. Others went off into the desert for solitary prayer and meditation (and perhaps to escape the atmosphere of power struggle that was already developing).

The First Ecumenical Council at Nicaea was convened (two hundred and ninety-five years after the Crucifixion) to gather up Christianity from the multitude of ideas and authorities that were then circulating, and tailor a Christianity that suited the World of the Greeks (as recently taken over by the Roman Emperor, Constantine). Christianity becomes an important element in civil government.

I think we may assume that Nicaea did not achieve the instantly unifying effect that was expected. Fifty-six years later, a second Ecumenical Council was called at Constantinople at which things were really tightened up. Nicaean Christianity was the only subject worthy of study: all else was to be discarded. Goodbye to literature, art and science!

Avoiding all this political re-ordering of the Christian Church, monks and hermits in the sands of Egypt and Syria maintained their quiet study and prayer.

It is probably true that monks and hermits from this desert tradition found their way to Ireland in the early 400's, so one can understand concern being felt back in Rome when they found out. There can't be two different sorts of Christianity; can there? Rome was descended from Saint Peter, and Saint Peter had been instructed by Jesus Christ himself, so Rome knew that they were right! Rome despatched an agent to bring the Irish monks into line.

But it didn't happen quite like that. The Irish monastic tradition went on developing, and in due course appeared in Scotland, Wales and England. Indeed, one might say, 'Yes — there are two different sorts of Christianity!' There is the Christianity of politically aware Constantinople and Rome, following rules set down by the Ecumenical Councils: and then there were monks of the Western world living an isolated and spiritual Christianity, with memories going back to the Egyptian desert and to authority in Alexandria.

The sixth century saw the Byzantine Emperor Justinian (527-565) become the leading figure in our story. He had ambitions to expand into the West and to re-establish the old Roman Empire, and he was successful in taking over control in Italy. (We remember that Italy had been in the hands of the Ostrogoths, a Christian group, but of the Arian sort.) Christian thinking at this time was seriously divided. Did Jesus have one nature or two? One divine nature — or two natures, one divine and the other human? The Fourth Ecumenical Council at Chalcedon had decided on two, but arguments persisted between Chalcedonians and Monophysites. Unfortunately, Justinian was a Chalcedonian, while his wife Theodora was a Mono. Justinian had a keen interest in theology and took part in debates on Christian doctrine. He also took the lead in bringing the old Roman Law Codes up to date. (Justinian is also, so far as I am aware, the only significant figure in history to catch bubonic plague, recover, and go back to work!)

By the time of Pope Gregory the Great (590-604) attention was now clearly focused on Rome. The Eastern Orthodoxy of Byzantium was dropping out of sight, so far as Western Europe was concerned.

Three great catastrophes await the Christian Church.

<u>Number 1</u>

The middle 600's see an enormous expansion of a new religion, Islam. Up to this point Christianity had been developing in Iraq and the Near East and was spreading eastwards across Asia. Almost overnight, the people of these lands became Muslims, and so did the people along the south coast of the Mediterranean. Christian thoughts of becoming a world-wide religion fell back to being a religion of Europe. Could it be that Islam saw all its members as equals under Mohammed, whereas Christians felt more like foot-soldiers at the bottom of a command structure?

Number 2

The relationship between Rome and Constantinople became ever more stretched. Rome carried on the expansionist ideas of its military forebears, while Constantinople turned in upon itself. Each excommunicated the other from time to time. Roman Christianity was now the religion of the western half of Europe.

Number 3

As already described in some detail, the 800's saw the destruction by the Vikings of the monastic element of Christianity in western Europe.

In the year 800 Charlemagne and Pope Leo had ideas about reconstructing Europe — something along the lines of a New Roman Empire; and at the same time, giving the Church a better organised framework. In 816 the monasteries were instructed to follow the Rule of Saint Benedict and somewhere in the early 800's the forged document known as the 'Donation of Constantine' began to circulate. But not a lot happened for the next century or so. (While Charlemagne's children and grandchildren squabbled.)

By the middle of the tenth century things were on the move. Energy originating with the Vikings was reshaping the politics of Europe, and although the Papacy itself was going through a 'low' period, religious ideas were being spread from the Abbey at Cluny. Cluniac ideas were leading the Christian Church along a path of greater display and elaborate ceremonies. In England, Dunstan was introducing these continental ideas into both Church and Monastery.

At this point I need to cross swords with many others who have written about this period. It is commonly implied that Dunstan's work, later to be supported and expanded by the wealth of the Norman lords, was a simple revival, or a re-introduction of the old ideas of Christian monasticism that had roots going back into the seventh, the sixth, or even the fifth century. NO. Monasticism before the Viking destruction was very different in a number of important ways from the monasticism that grew in the tenth and eleventh centuries from seeds planted by Charlemagne and Leo.

Pre-Viking monasticism was on a small scale: a handful of monks living in a group of simple buildings out in the wilds of somewhere. Isolation was important. They were the seed from which God's work would spread into the wider community.

The monastic tradition brought into England in the tenth century was very different. It was on a far larger scale. Indeed, some have made comparisons with an army barracks, with order, discipline and a firm attachment to Rome. (Re-read the early part of Chapter Thirteen.)

At this point, we join up with the tales of monastic life as told in our history books, with monasteries providing food and shelter for travellers, comfort and a proper bed for the sick, and a simple education for those that asked. If your choice fell on a different history book, you might read of monks sliding into easy living while the lay brothers did the work; of monastic houses becoming enormously rich as men frightened by tales of purgatory and hell, donated part of their land to the Church. Increasing wealth seems to spark an urge for even more, and schemes were devised to inflate Church income. From this point we can see the way to Reformation!

SOME LEFT-OVER THOUGHTS

At this stage, and not for the first time, I feel I owe the reader an apology. My chosen title suggests a content of 50% religion, but in so many cases, a story that starts with religion slides downhill into civil government, politics and money. Perhaps this is, in itself, a lesson.

EPILOGUE

> God be in my head,
>> And in my understanding;
>
> God be in my eyes,
>> And in my looking;
>
> God be in my mouth,
>> And in my speaking;
>
> God be in my heart,
>> And in my thinking;
>
> God be at my end,
>> And at my departing.
>
> (Hymns Ancient & Modern)

Christianity has been with us for just over, or just under two thousand years. (Depending upon your view of the Nativity scenes.) Theologians may insist that the Faith of today is the same as it was at the beginning: this may well be true, but Nicaea saw faith blended with Government, and Government has to follow the changing patterns of human life. Thus today, we have bishops in Parliament and our bottom level of local government is called the Parish Council. We all know the church at the end of the road — it's where we turn left to get to the shops. And is there anyone out there who doesn't know the date for Christmas? Christianity is built into everyday life. There are some who try to live a more actively Christian life, but their number seems to be declining. The idea that Christianity drew people together and gave them a common framework up which they could grow — seems to have been overtaken by the Smartphone.

Christianity set itself up to communicate with the whole world (or as much of the world as it could gather under its wing). Thus it found itself facing the whole range of human variety, from A plus to D minus. The Church's main solution to this situation was to lay emphasis on faith; for faith carries a special magic that enables it to work at all levels, from dozy to bright. Faith also has the happy knack of side-stepping around those awkward questions, "Is it true?" "Is it right?". So successful has the Church been, that for many people 'Faith' and 'Religion' are the same thing (and they might even be right!). Faith offers comfort at times of fear and at times of loss; it shines a light on our ideas of right and wrong and it is difficult to argue with a man of faith; he just smiles and says, "This is what I believe." Unfortunately, when Faiths clash, there is seldom a simple solution for faith and logic follow different paths.

But there is something else. Something hard to see: hard to understand. Where words are but pointers. A sermon may talk of mind, of soul and of spirit, and if we are lucky, we might understand the world to which they point. As some scripture, somewhere, says, "Lord give us luck!" Or, as a famous golfer once said, "The more I practice, the luckier I get!" It has just occurred to me that this 'luck', this 'Light on the horizon', this gift of God, is the same thing that tipped Saint Augustine into depression. What I have seen as luck and as a route towards understanding, Augustine saw as a God-controlled world in which he was no more than a pawn in God's game.

What, then, of this 'other' sort of Christianity? I quote my favourite among the sayings of Jesus, "Become passers-by." This, clearly, is not telling us to walk past on the other side of the road without noticing. It tells us to live life to the full: to earn a living; to raise a family and to live a full life of enjoyment mixed with other things (for were there not 'other things', we would not notice the enjoyment!). Having enjoyed the enjoyment, do not get stuck, move on: become passers-by: other things may await. One of the things that may await is understanding, and while you are 'standing under' you might look up and see how the world really works. One thing you might notice is that you are not alone: many have followed this path; thinkers from a variety of traditions. Christianity has been a tributary bringing you to a wider river. It is difficult to wade through deep water, but there are things to help.

> "The Dharma that I have found is profound, hard to see, hard to understand; it is peaceful, sublime, beyond the sphere of mere reasoning, subtle, to be experienced by the wise."
>
> (Dharma is the divine law underlying reality, or, if you prefer Socrates, 'the realm of Forms.')

There are many passages of this sort and the rule is simple; if you find them helpful, use them. If you don't, let them go. Who wrote them, or when, is not important. Use your own judgement.

> "From your own kitchen window you may see the way to heaven."

EPILOGUE

Let me finish with a story: a story that has stuck in my mind for more than seventy years — there was once a popular magazine called 'Photoplay', concerned with cinema and the world of film people. Somewhere in the early 1940's I read about a famous film actor who was telling a story from his childhood: -

> He was out walking with his father when they saw a blind man begging at the roadside. The father gave his son a penny to go and give to the beggar. On his return, the father said, "Why did you not raise your hat?" To which the son replied, "But the beggar was blind: he would not have noticed." The father's response, "Go back and raise your hat — he might be an imposter!"

INDEX

Abba Moses, 56
Abraham, 33, 34
Act of Supremacy, 96
Acts of the Apostles, 106
Adam and Eve, 54, 66
Adonai, 34
Aethelred the Unready, 125, 130, 131
Agincourt, 86
Alan Gemmell (Professor), 6
Alban (see under Saint)
Albigensian Crusade, 22
Alexandria, 33, 46, 56, 62, 70, 71, 72, 73, 74, 78, 112, 116, 140, 174
Alfred (King), 124, 128
Allah, 28, 121
Ambrose (Bishop of Milan), 20, 49, 140
Amos, 34
Anglo-Saxon raiders, 83, 140
Anne Askew, 98
Anne Boleyn, 2, 6, 24, 94
Antioch, 46, 62, 70, 72, 74, 116
Antony (Hermit), 53, 56, 79, 164
Apostles, 37, 39, 64, 106, 107
Apostolic Succession, 37
Arius and the Arians, 48, 62, 71, 109, 173
Arthur (King), 83, 93, 94
Assyrians, 35
Athanasius, 56
Athelstan (King), 58, 85, 125
Augustine (of England), 6, 9, 51, 53, 55, 57, 58, 66, 67, 75, 82, 83, 84, 85, 100, 134, 179
Augustine (of Hippo), 49, 140, 154

Bartholomew (Apostle), 38
Bede (The Venerable), 75
Berlin Gnostic Codex, 10
Bethlehem, 1, 8, 36, 65
Bishop of Lincoln, 16
Bishop of Winchester, 23
Bishops - creation of, 37, 45, 46
Black Death (Bubonic Plague), 17, 19, 42, 43, 158, 161, 162
Black Ogre, 93
Bogomils, 21
Bosworth Field, 92, 93, 168
Buddhist Nirvana, 11

Canaan, 33
Canute (King), 125, 131, 134
Cathars, 21
Catherine of Aragon, 6, 89, 94, 95
Cats of Heresy, 51
Charlemagne, 115, 116, 117, 121, 122, 124, 127, 128, 132, 134, 135, 139, 141, 144, 145, 154, 166, 168, 175, 176
Charles V, 86, 94, 95
China, 73, 109, 118, 165
Choir Nuns, 155
Church building, 161, 162
Church Fathers, 48, 72
Church of St Peter, 65
Church of the East, 47, 72, 73
Church of the Holy Apostles of Jesus, 64
Church of the Holy Sepulchre, 65
Church of the Nativity, 65
Clocks (Invention of), 154

Cluny (Abbey), 134, 141, 142, 145, 149, 151, 153, 154, 155, 172, 176
Columba, 57, 82, 140
Compostela (St James of), 50
Constantine (Emperor), 5, 6, 15, 20, 23, 29, 40, 42, 43, 44, 45, 46, 50, 59, 60, 61, 63, 64, 65, 68, 71, 73, 76, 80, 87, 92, 100, 108, 109, 111, 112, 117, 139, 143, 144, 146, 157, 165, 171, 173
Constantine's Mother, 5
Constantinople/Byzantium, 15, 20, 22, 23, 42, 43, 46, 48, 60, 62, 64, 67, 69, 70, 71, 72, 73, 74, 78, 81, 84, 87, 92, 109, 112, 115, 165, 166, 171, 173, 174, 175
Constantius II, 68
Coptic Church, 56, 73, 81
Council of Arles (314), 58, 76
       Chalcedon (451), 140
       Constance (1415), 91
       Constantinople (381), 15
       Ephesus (431), 46
       Ephesus (449), 47
       Nicaea (325), 15, 21, 64, 67, 100, 109
       Trent (1546), 36, 163
Creation of the World, 29, 143
Crocodile, 8
Crucifixion, The, 35, 39, 103, 104, 108
Crusades, 90, 149
Culloden battlefield, 25
Cyrenius (Governor of Syria), 100
Cyril (Bishop of Alexandria), 46, 47

Danegelt, 125
David (King), 4, 76, 82, 101, 118
Dead Sea Scrolls, 12, 33
Defender of the Faith, 89, 99
Desert Fathers, 9, 11, 56, 79
Devil, 21
Diocletian, 59, 76, 108
Discourse on the Eighth and Ninth, 10
Divorce (Henry VIII), 6, 24, 94, 95, 96
Donation of Constantine, 74, 175
Doubting Thomas, 38
Duality, 62

Easter (Date of), 57, 81
Ecumenical Councils, 47, 174
Edict of Milan, 59, 62, 77, 108
Edward the Confessor, 131, 134, 135, 137
Egyptian Obelisk, 112
Elizabeth of York, 92
Enlightenment, 10
Erasmus, 41
Eric Bloodaxe, 85
Escape from Egypt, 33
Eschatology, 170
Eusebius (Bishop), 60, 61
Eve, 54, 66
Exodus, 32, 34

Ferdinand (King of Spain), 89, 169
Fountains Abbey, 155
French Church, 88
Friars, 154, 156, 158
Fulford (Battle), 136, 137

Gallarus Oratory, 79, 80
Garden of Eden, 21, 54, 66, 144

Geoffrey Chaucer, 19, 24, 159
Germain (Saint), 57, 58, 80, 139
Gillian Evans, 16, 36
Gnostic beliefs and writings, 10, 11, 21, 25, 62, 111
Gospel of Mary, 10
Gospel of Thomas, 9, 171
Gospels (dates of), 16, 28, 35, 37, 48, 100, 101, 103, 104
Great Schism, 20, 87, 159, 163
Gynaecology, 55

Harald Hardrada, 135, 136, 137
Haran, 33
Harold Godwinson, 135, 136, 137
Harrying of the North, 138
Heaven, 21, 53, 55, 89, 140, 163
Helena (Mother of Constantine), 65
Hell, 90
Hengist and Horsa, 83
Henry III (Emperor), 129
Henry VII (King), 92
Henry VIII (King), 2, 6, 29, 43, 86, 91, 92, 93, 95, 96, 98, 100, 159, 163, 168, 169
Herding Cats, 48
Heresies, 45, 52, 68, 112, 114
Hermes, 10
Herod (King), 1, 100, 102, 103
Herod Agrippa, 38
Herod Antipas, 102
Highland Clearances, 89, 156
Hilda (Abbess), 58
Hindu Religion, 55, 56
Hinton St Mary (Dorset), 76
Holy Ghost, 62, 64, 87, 111
Holy Roman Empire, 117, 141, 166
Homoousios, 64
Honorius (Emperor), 70

Hosea, 34
Huneric (King of the Vandals), 71

Immaculate Conception, 54, 66
Indian teacher, 26
Indulgencies, 88, 89, 90, 163
Iona, 57, 58, 82, 84, 140
Ireland, 56, 57, 58, 79, 80, 81, 82, 84, 85, 139, 173
Irene (Empress), 116
Isaiah, 34
Islam, 4, 116, 118, 120, 121, 151, 174
Islamic expansion, 73, 118, 119, 121, 140, 151, 169
Israel, 33, 34, 35, 101, 107

James (son of Zebedee), 38
Jan Hus, 20, 24, 91, 160, 164
Jehovah, 34
Jerome (Saint), 8, 36, 41, 67, 68, 139
Jihad, 119
John of Gaunt, 88
John Wycliff, 16, 20, 24, 43, 88, 90, 91, 164
Joseph of Arimathea, 75, 104
Josephus, 107
Judas Iscariot, 38
Judas Maccabaeus, 101
Judas Thomas, 9
Julian (The Apostate), 68
Justinian (Emperor), 174

King James Version, 31, 32
Koran, 28, 118, 120, 121, 151

Lanfranc (Archbishop), 135, 146, 149
Licinius (co-Emperor), 59, 60
Life after Death, 170

Lindisfarne, 1, 57, 82, 84, 132, 140, 149, 172
Llantwit Major, 82
Lourdes, 133
Lucius (King), 76, 134
Lullingstone Villa, 77

Magic and Witchcraft, 98
Magna Carta, 32
Manichaean Heresy, 49
Mare's milk, 73
Marriage customs, 147, 148
Martin Luther, 95, 163, 166
Martyrs, 53, 105, 133, 160
Mary (The Virgin), 44, 71, 75
Mary of Magdala, 11
Masoretic Text, 33
Matthias, 38
Maxentius, 59
Merchant of Venice, 29
Merneptah, 33
Merv (Turkmenistan), 72
Micah, 34
Milvian Bridge, 59, 61, 108, 169
Miracles, 27, 28
Mohammed, 28, 118, 119, 120, 121, 175
Monastic sites of early foundation, 82
Money economy, 126
Moses, 31, 32
Mount Sinai, 34
Mouse, 39
Move from Greece to Rome, 16, 48, 78, 108, 109
Move from Rome to Greece, 109
Muslims, 28, 42, 51, 119, 120, 121, 126, 149, 151, 175
Myrrh, 104
Mystery (The medieval sense of), 110

Nag Hammadi, 9, 10, 11
National Health Service, 7
Nero, 39, 105
Nestorian Church, 72
Nestorius (Bishop), 46, 47, 71, 72, 80
Nicaea (see Council of)
Nicene Creed, 63, 112
Nicodemus, 104
Nuns, 18, 43, 79, 155

Obelisk of Thutmoses III, 112
Oddities (about the crucifixion), 103
Odoacer, 114
Olympic Games, 112
Omri, 33
Origen, 78
Original Sin, 55, 148
Oxford University, 16, 17, 18, 91, 156
Oxyrhynchus, 8

Palladius, 57, 58, 81, 139
Papacy (Low period), 129, 133
Patriarchates, 70
Peasants Revolt, 138
Pelagius, 67, 80, 91, 139
Philistines, 4, 33
Pontius Pilate, 27, 102
Pope Alexander II (1061-1073), 135, 146
   Alexander VI (1492-1503), 88
   Benedict IX (1032-1048), 129
   Boniface IX (1389-1404), 88
   Celestine (422-432), 57, 58, 80, 81, 139
   Clement VII (1378-1394), 20, 159
   Clement VII/2 (1523-1534), 94, 95

Damasus (366-384), 36, 68
Eleutherius (174-189), 76
Formosus (891-896), 129
Gregory the Great (590-604), 11, 48, 51, 166, 174
Hadrian (772-795), 1
Innocent III (1198-1216), 21
John XII (955-963), 134
John XXIII (1410-1415), 20
John Paul II (1978-2005), 47
Julius II (1503-1513),
Leo (440-461), 47, 73, 109, 117, 128, 139, 154
Leo III (795-816), 117, 134, 166
Leo X (1513-1521), 94, 99
Paul VI (1963-1978), 39
Pius XII (1939-1958), 87
Sylvester (314-335), 74, 129
Urban II (1088-1099), 90, 149
Urban VI (1378-1389), 20, 88, 159
Predestination, 67
Primogeniture, 86
Priscillian (Bishop), 49, 50
Prophets, 32, 34, 35
Purgatory, 19, 87, 88, 90, 152, 163

Reading and Writing, 132
Realm of Forms, 31, 180
Red Wall Complex, 39
Reformation, 24, 43, 44, 52, 95, 96, 97, 99, 146, 163, 164, 165, 176
Richard III's bones, 92

Ritual, 14, 44, 145
Ritual Pit, 14
Robert Browning, 30
Rollo (Viking leader), 128
Rule of St Benedict, 139
Rus, 125

Saint Alban, 76, 139
Dunstan, 133, 134, 151, 154, 176
Illtud, 82, 140
Ninian, 79, 82, 140
Patrick, 81, 140
Paul, 8, 104, 106, 107, 108, 172
Peter, 38, 39, 42, 85, 99, 108, 130, 145, 165, 173
Saint Brice's Day Massacre, 125
Saint Peter's Basilica, 25, 39
Santiago de Compostela, 38, 50
Septuagint, 33
Servant Nuns, 155
Seth and Sophia, 10
Sex, 36, 54
Sheep farming, 23, 156
Simeon Stylites, 56
Skellig Michael, 79, 81
Slaves, 50, 122, 126, 138, 147
Socrates and Plato, 31, 51, 61, 112
Sol Invictus, 60, 61
Spanish Inquisition, 89
Stamford Bridge (Battle), 136, 137
Statute of Six Articles, 97
Sunni and Shia Muslims, 120
Swein Forkbeard, 125, 131
Synod of Whitby, 58, 85, 140
Syriac Church, 8, 41, 42, 72

Tetragrammaton, 34
Theodosian Rule, 71, 113

Theodosius (Emperor), 42, 46, 69, 112, 140
Theodosius II, 46, 72
Thorkell the Tall, 131
Thunder god, 14
Tight-fitting suit, 51
Torture, 22, 49, 50, 70, 151, 171
Transubstantiation, 7, 98, 151
Trinity, 21, 23, 63, 64, 65, 70, 75, 111, 112
True Cross, 5, 65

Valentinus, 10
Venerable Bede, 75, 79
Vestal Virgins, 112
Vikings, 1, 22, 82, 122, 123, 124, 125, 126, 127, 128, 129, 130, 132, 141, 142, 153, 154, 160, 166, 168, 175
Viking World View, 123, 143, 144
Vladimir (Prince), 126
Vortigern (King), 83
Vulgate, 36, 40, 41, 42, 43, 67, 68

Westminster Abbey, 135, 137
Whithorn (Scotland), 79, 82
William Duke of Normandy, 128, 136, 137, 138, 139, 143
William of Malmesbury, 149
William Tyndale, 91
Winchester Geese, 23
Women and their status, 53, 73, 133, 148
Word of God, 24, 31, 35, 36, 40
World Council of Churches, 57
World of Form, 31, 152
Year 381 (see also the Council of Constantinople), 2
Year 597 (see also Augustine), 75
Year 1000, 130, 168
Year 1066, 134, 137, 139
YHWH, 33, 34

Zealots, 102
Zen Buddhist exercise, 66
Zeus/Jupiter, 7
Zoroastrianism, 118

www.ingramcontent.com/pod-product-compliance
Lightning Source LLC
Chambersburg PA
CBHW042235090526

44589CB00001B/1